The Odes of Horace

Johns Hopkins
New Translations
from Antiquity

# The Odes of Horace

Translated by Jeffrey H. Kaimowitz

Introduction by Ronnie Ancona

The Johns Hopkins University Press
Baltimore

© 2008 The Johns Hopkins University Press
All rights reserved. Published 2008
Printed in the United States of America on acid-free paper
9 8 7 6 5 4 3 2 1

The Johns Hopkins University Press
2715 North Charles Street
Baltimore, Maryland 21218-4363
www.press.jhu.edu

Library of Congress Cataloging-in-Publication Data

Horace.
  [Carmina. English]
  The odes of Horace / translated by Jeffrey H. Kaimowitz ; introduction by Ronnie Ancona.
    p. cm.
  ISBN-13: 978-0-8018-8995-0 (hardcover : alk. paper)
  ISBN-10: 0-8018-8995-2 (hardcover : alk. paper)
  ISBN-13: 978-0-8018-8996-7 (pbk. : alk. paper)
  ISBN-10: 0-8018-8996-0 (pbk. : alk. paper)
  1. Horace—Translations into English. 2. Laudatory poetry, Latin—Translations into
English. 3. Verse satire, Latin—Translations into English. 4. Rome—Poetry. I. Kaimowitz,
Jeffrey H. II. Title.
  PA6395.K35 2008
  874'.01—dc22        2008007275

A catalog record for this book is available from the British Library.

*Special discounts are available for bulk purchases of this book. For more information, please
contact Special Sales at 410-516-6936 or specialsales@press.jhu.edu.*

The Johns Hopkins University Press uses environmentally friendly book materials,
including recycled text paper that is composed of at least 30 percent post-consumer
waste, whenever possible. All of our book papers are acid-free, and our jackets and covers
are printed on paper with recycled content.

# Contents

Preface  vii

Translator's Note  ix

Introduction, by Ronnie Ancona  xvii

**The Odes of Horace**  1

Book I  3

Book II  55

Book III  89

Book IV  143

# Preface

Still another translation of Horace's *Odes*? Yes, because in this metrical translation I hope to have brought something new to the ever quixotic challenge of trying to render Horace's inimitable lyric poems in English. All the versions are offered in verse schemes reminiscent of Horace's meters but firmly based on English prosody; I comment on metrics at greater length in the Translator's Note. My goal has been literary. The translations are intended as poems in their own right. Though I have worked to keep as close to the original as possible, literary values, including metrical discipline, lead to results that are not always literal. For example, references are sometimes modified for the sake of more immediate clarity and comprehension and are occasionally omitted entirely, if I feel this can be done without sacrificing the overall meaning and movement of the poem. The basic Latin text I have employed is the fifth edition of Horace's works, edited by F. Klingner and published by Teubner. A list of points in the *Odes* where I have used readings other than those of Klingner appears at the end of the Translator's Note. To facilitate comprehension and accessibility, I have annotated the translation throughout, explaining various references. The notes are generally not intended to be interpretative; the textual choices and the translation itself seem interpretation enough. For the sake of convenience, annotation for a name or topic that appears more than once is usually repeated or provided with a cross reference.

There are many whose help I have enjoyed during the genesis of this translation. The late Hugh Ogden and the late Millie Silvestri were very supportive in the early stages of the project. I also appreciate the encouragement I received from the editors of *Classical World*, the *Formalist*, and *Connecticut Review* by their publication of versions of the translations in their journals. Jayne Gaebel and Robert Gaebel each carefully read and commented on the completed translation, and Robert Palter similarly read and commented on the first two books, and for this I owe all three of them a great debt. In addition, the comments of the Johns Hopkins Press's outside reader were extremely helpful. I also want to thank Michael Lonegro, acquisitions editor for humanities and ancient studies at the Johns Hopkins University Press, for championing this translation; Ronnie Ancona, for her fine introduction, which so beautifully contextualizes and introduces Horace and his poetry; and Barbara Lamb, for her expert copyediting. Most of all, I am grateful to my wonderful wife, Llyn, with whom I have shared over the years many of the drafts of the poems and whose encouragement, patience, and hardheaded feedback have been of inestimable help.

# Translator's Note

## Reading the *Odes*

The *Odes* of Horace present a complex array of subjects and influences. The varied themes include a great deal about the enjoyment of life and aware-ness of its evanescence, friendship, amorous love and hate, patriotic reflec-tions on the Roman state, mythology, the beauty and simplicity of country life, the poetic vocation, and all this through the lens of Horace's often bemused but sympathetic eye. There is also the panoply of Greek authors who influenced Horace's writing, explicitly and implicitly, including his innovations in metrics, unique in its range and extent in Roman poetry. Thus he makes frequent mention of Aeolic poetry, song native to the island of Lesbos, whose two great exponents were Alcaeus and Sappho. He also refers to the delicate poetry of Anacreon of Teos and to the powerful verse of the great choral poet Pindar of Thebes, whose influence is crucial in the complex architecture of many of Horace's poems. At the same time, the influence of the themes and sophisticated pose of Hellenistic Greek poetry, notably the epigram, though not acknowledged explicitly, is evident in many of the *Odes*, as well as the influence of Hellenistic philosophy, notably Epicureanism and Stoicism. Though striking out on a new departure for Roman poetry, Horace's work also reflects the influence of distinguished Latin writers who were his predecessors and contemporaries—writers like Ennius, Catullus, Lucretius, Vergil, and the writers of Roman elegy.

One of the most attractive and striking characteristics of Horace's poetry is his use of language. Horace's ideals in writing are evident in the verse itself, but we are also fortunate to have his explicit statement of what he valued in his art, particularly with regard to diction and word placement, in his literary epistles, especially the last of the series, *Epistle* II.3, *The Art of Poetry*. Here are two revealing passages:[1]

> Take material, would-be writers, suited to your
> strength and ponder long what your shoulders will and will not

---

1. The translation is my own; the text follows D. R. Shackleton Bailey's edition (Stuttgart: Teubner, 1985), but without emending *potenter* (according to his talents) to *pudenter* (with a proper sense of restraint) in line 40; see the commentary of Niall Rudd in *Horace Epistles, Book II, and Epistle to the Pisones* (*'Ars Poetica'*) (Cambridge: Cambridge University Press, 1989), 155–56.

bear. Who chooses a subject according to his talents
will lack neither eloquence nor lucid order.
Force and charm of order derive from this (if I am
not mistaken) in saying now what must be said now
and deferring and omitting much for the present.
Let the author of a promised poem favor
this, reject that. Also by spare and careful entwining
of words, your diction will be splendid, if canny
collocation makes a well-known word new.
(38–48)

And again:

I will pursue a song that's shaped from the familiar,
so that any may hope to do the same—and struggle
much in vain attempt. So very powerful are flow and
collocation, so honored is use of our common word stock.
(240–43)

Horace's use of language, especially his "mosaic of words," to use Nietz-
sche's phrase, is one of the most characteristic and most untranslatable
features of his poetry. Take the opening lines of the Pyrrha Ode (I.5): "Quis
multa gracilis te puer in rosa" (What slight young man [pursues] you on
many a rose).[2] In the Latin, "What young man" (Quis . . . puer) surrounds
"many" (multa), "slight" (gracilis) and "you" (te) and is followed by "on a
rose" (in rosa), making for a sophisticatedly tentative opening of mild sur-
prise, which is only clear at the end of the line and then only partially, for
the word "pursues" (urget) does not appear until the next line.

## Translating Horace

If the old expression traduttore, traditore (translator, traitor) is true and
all translations betray to some degree their originals, then in their trea-
son, translators of poetry should at least provide something approaching
poetry. I have tried to maintain a modern but dignified tone throughout
the translations, believing this to be consonant with the spirit of Horace's
lyric poetry. I avoided colloquialisms and, without sacrificing sense, made
an effort to be concise—I hope, in a characteristically Horatian manner.
As already noted, in English, with its analytic syntax and lack of inflections,

---

2. This version of the first line is a little more literal than that employed in my actual trans-
lation of this ode.

the striking kinds of effect that Horace achieved in word placement are usually impossible, but throughout, I have tried to impart movement and to avoid the prosaic and, when possible, to imitate the emphasis achieved by Horatian word placement.

A major aspect of Horace's success is his virtuosity with metrics. Therefore, in translating highly structured metrical verse such as Horace writes, formal meter seems essential if something reflecting the concision and force of the original is to be approximated. For this reason, metrics have a central role in this translation. The verse of Horace is written in strict lyric meters adapted from the early Greek poetic tradition, notably, verse forms associated with Alcaeus and Sappho, who composed their poetry in their local Greek dialect, Aeolic. Classical meter, however, is quantitative, that is, based on a succession of long and short syllables, a metrical system not readily adaptable to English prosody, which is based principally on syllable stress and falls naturally into either an iambic (u_) or a trochaic pattern (_u). To try to employ a quantitative system in English constitutes a tremendous straitjacket to communicating the meaning and movement of a poem.

The verse systems employed in my translations are, in general, regular metrically and reminiscent of the Horatian meters but do not attempt actually to reproduce them. In devising my metrical "reminiscences," my main concern has been to insure that the verse flow easily but in a disciplined manner from line to line, with sufficient syllables to encompass the content to be conveyed. At the same time, these metrical "reminiscences," which are used consistently throughout the whole translation, are parallel to the Horatian meters in having the same number of lines, with the same or a similar number of syllables per line, and with the progression of stressed and unstressed syllables paralleling to a degree the progression of long and short syllables in the original classical meter.[3] For this reason, I have felt justified in naming the original meter, upon which my reminiscence is based, in connection with each poem, in order to illustrate the variety of metrical schemata that Horace employs.

A few examples of the many metrical schemes employed by Horace side by side with the reminiscence will exemplify my method of adaptation. In Latin, "u" indicates a short syllable, and in English, an unstressed syllable. In Latin, "_" is a long syllable, and in English, a stressed syllable.

---

3. The adaptations of the various Asclepiad stanzas are consistent throughout the translation, but the glyconic line (_ _ _ u u _ u u), which is employed as one of the lines in constituting the second, third, and fourth Asclepiad stanzas, is adapted differently in the each of the stanzas.

*Alcaic stanza*

U _ U _ _ // _ U U _ U U
U _ U _ _ // _ U U _ U U
   U _ U _ _ _ U _ U
    _ U U _ U U _ U _ U

*Alcaic stanza (reminiscence)*

U _ U _U_ U _ U _
U _ U _U_ U _ U _
   U _ U _U_ U _ U
    _ U _U_ U _ U

*Sapphic stanza*

_ U _ _ _ // U U _ U _ U
_ U _ _ _ // U U _ U _ U
_ U _ _ _ // U U _ U _ U
   _ U U _ U

*Sapphic stanza (reminiscence)*

_ U _ U _U _ U _ U
_ U _ U _U _ U _ U
_ U _ U _U _ U _ U
   _ U U _ U

*Third Asclepiad system*

_ _ _ U U _ // _ U U _ U U
_ _ _ U U _ // _ U U _ U U
   _ _ _ U U _ U
    _ _ _ U U _ U U

*Third Asclepiad system (reminiscence)*

U _ U _ U_ U _ U _
U _ U _ U_ U _ U _
   U _ U _ U_ U
    _ U _ U_ U _

I should note that certain liberties, when deemed unavoidable, have been taken in employing these metrical reminiscences. As a principle, the four-line stanza, not the individual line within each stanza, is regarded as the metrical unit, and when a word at the end of a line has too many or too few syllables to fit metrically within the line, a metrical foot may be "borrowed from" or "lent to" the next line. Occasionally this even occurs between stanzas. For poems in the first and fifth Asclepiad systems, which have only one type of line, such "borrowing" is employed without restriction. Also, at sense pauses, an unstressed syllable may be dropped, though as a rule, when this happens, it does not happen more than once in a line. An example of these irregularities can be found in the fourth and fifth lines of the first ode of Book I:

> Olympic dust in chariots, avoiding
> turn posts with swift wheels: earthly lords

where the unstressed "ing" of "avoiding" in line four is borrowed from line five and where the unstressed syllable before "earthly" is omitted. Also, the last line in the Sapphic stanza, though always having five syllables, varies in stress at times, though the preferred pattern of a dactyl (_ U U) followed by a trochee (_ U) is maintained wherever possible.

Let me conclude with a few comments on pronunciation, especially accent—a crucial factor in reading this translation. Names in Latin, whether native or foreign, are *never* accented on their last syllable. To facilitate pronunciation, all uncommon proper names of more than two syllables have an accent on their stressed syllable. One should also note that in words ending in *-ium* and *-ius,* not infrequently the *i* is to be pronounced as consonantal *y,* as in the English word *yes:* thus, *Látium* and *Ílion* are pronounced with two syllables, as *Látyum* (or, more commonly, *Lashum*) and *Ílyon,* and *Fabrícius* and *Cúrius* as *Fabrícyus* and *Cúryus.* In addition, names like *Colchians* and *Dacians,* unless accented on their first syllable, are pronounced with two syllables. Also, frequently words with a weak internal syllable are to be pronounced without that syllable, as is common in everyday English, for example, *funeral* (two syllables) and *generously* (three syllables). In cases where a stronger syllable is dropped, the omission is indicated by the insertion of an apostrophe. With words ending in *s,* the addition of a possessive *s* means an additional syllable is to be sounded. The want of the additional *s* in such a case, where only an apostrophe indicates possession, indicates that no additional syllable is to be sounded.

Diphthongs, two adjacent vowel sounds pronounced together, also call for comment. The diphthongs that appear in names in the translations are pronounced as follows:

ae  as in *eye*

au  as *ow* in *now*

ei  as *ei* in *eight*

eu  ĕh-oo as one sound. Thus the name *Orpheus* or *Nereus* has only two syllables. A common pronunciation of this diphthong is *yus.*

oe  as *oy* in *boy,* though in common English pronunciation in the name *Phoebus, oe* is pronounced *ee.*

The key point is that these combined sounds all yield one syllable, never two. When a syllable with a diphthong is accented, the accent mark is placed over the second vowel.

When two consecutive vowels are to be pronounced separately, a diaeresis (two dots) is placed over the second vowel. An example is the name *Leucónoë,* where the first syllable is a diphthong, while the last two vowels are pronounced separately.

## Bibliographical and Textual Note

In preparing this translation, several commentaries were of central importance. These include the following annotated editions: T. E. Page's *Q. Horatii Flacci Carminum Libri IV; Epodon Liber, Edited with an Introduction and Notes* (1895; repr., London: Macmillan; New York: St. Martin's Press, 1967), Clement Lawrence Smith's *The Odes and Epodes of Horace, Edited with an Introduction and Notes,* 2nd ed. (Boston, Ginn & Co., 1904), Kenneth Quinn's *Horace, the Odes, Edited with an Introduction, Revised Text, and Commentary* (1980; repr., London: Bristol Classical Press, 2001), R. G. M. Nisbet and Margaret Hubbard's *A Commentary on Horace: Odes, Book I* (Oxford: Clarendon Press, 1970) and *A Commentary on Horace: Odes, Book II* (Oxford: Clarendon Press, 1978) [= N-H], R. G. M. Nisbet and Niall Rudd's *A Commentary on Horace: Odes, Book III* (Oxford: Oxford University Press, 2004) [= N-R], *Third Book of Horace's Odes, Edited with Translation and Running Commentary* by Gordon Williams (1969; repr., Oxford: Clarendon Press, 1987), and David West's *Horace Odes III, Dulce Periculum* (Oxford: Oxford University Press, 2002). Also of great help were L. P. Wilkinson's *Horace and His Lyric Poetry* (1951; repr., Cambridge: Cambridge University Press, 1968) and *Golden Latin Artistry* (1963; repr., Cambridge: Cambridge University Press, 1966), Eduard Fraenkel, *Horace* (1957; repr., Oxford: Oxford University Press, 1997), D. R. Shackleton Bailey's *Profile of Horace* (Cambridge, MA: Harvard University Press, 1982), and Michael C. J. Putnam's *Artifices of Eternity: Horace's Fourth Book of Odes* (Ithaca, NY: Cornell University Press, 1986). One of the pleasures of doing this translation has been the opportunity to become intimate with these fine works of scholarship, which have contributed so much to my efforts. Any deficiencies in the translations are of course entirely my own.

The basic text used for this translation is that of Klingner (Leipzig: Teubner, 1970) [= K], with additional readings from the text of D. R. Shackleton Bailey (Stuttgaut: Teubner, 1985) [= SB], Nisbet and Hubbard's commentaries on Books I and II, and Nisbet and Rudd's commentary on Book III. In the list below, I have indicated the major places where I have employed a reading different from Klingner's. All readers of ancient texts in translation should understand that no ancient author's work is free of textual problems. Because the texts were transmitted over a long period in manuscript form, casual errors and purposeful alterations inevitably entered the textual tradition. This is not to say that ancient texts are riddled with problems, though some texts are much more problematic than others, but, even with the continuous efforts of brilliant textual critics, an unavoidable baggage of uncertainty will remain.

## Variations from the Text of Klingner

| | | | | |
|---|---|---|---|---|
| I.8.6 | equitat | | III.14.6 | divis |
| I.8.7 | temperat | | III.14.11 | non |
| I.28.21 | rabidus | | III.14.22 | cohibente |
| I.31.10 | et | | III.19.12 | miscentor |
| I.32.15 | medicumque | | III.20.8 | illi |
| I.34.5 | relectos | | III.21.10 | negleget |
| I.36.6 | dividit | | III.24.4 | Tyrrhenum |
| II.1.21 | videre | | III.24.30 | carus |
| II.2.14 | pellas | | III.24.44 | deserere |
| II.13.23 | descriptas | | III.24.54 | firmandae |
| II.15.13 | probatus | | III.26.7 | securesque |
| II.18.32 | Erum quid | | IV.2.13 | -ve |
| III.4.4 | -que | | IV.2.49 | tuque |
| III.4.46 | umbras | | IV.5.31 | tecta |
| III.4.47 | turbas | | IV.9.8 | -ve |
| III.8.26 | *delete* et | | | |

# Introduction
## *Ronnie Ancona*

## Horace's Life and Times

The Latin poet Quintus Horatius Flaccus, known to English speakers as Horace (this is the Anglicized version of his *nomen*, or family name), was born on 8 December 65 BCE, in the town of Venusia, located in the border area between the southern Italian regions of Apulia and Lucania. He died on 27 November 8 BCE, in the city of Rome. He and Vergil are the best known Latin poets from the second half of the first century BCE. Our knowledge of Horace comes primarily from two sources. The first is Horace's own writings. These, of course, due to the circular nature of self-reference, like those of any writer, need to be used with caution as a source on their own author. The second is a short biography of him, which has come down to us in the history of literary transmission along with some of the manuscripts of his writings. This biography is probably a version of the life of Horace written by the biographer Suetonius (b. ca. 69 CE) for *De Poetis (Concerning Poets)*, a section of his work *De Viris Illustribus (Concerning Illustrious Men)*, his collection of lives of Roman literary figures.

Horace's name, itself, is preserved for us in his own writings as well as in an inscription that still exists, which records Horace's composition of a poem known in Latin as the *carmen saeculare,* or centennial hymn. This poem was commissioned especially for the Secular Games of 17 BCE, held by the emperor Augustus. These games were a Roman celebration marking the end of one age, or *saeculum,* and the beginning of the next. They had not been held at Rome for over a century. It would have been a great honor to Horace to have been the poet asked to write for this occasion. The hymn was performed by a chorus of boys and girls, first at the newly built temple of Apollo on the Palatine hill, and then on the Capitoline hill, or Capitolium, the religious center of Rome. It featured many figures important to Rome, including Apollo, the god with whom Augustus closely associated himself.

The century in which Horace lived and died saw the end of the Roman Republic and the beginning of the Roman Empire. The emperor Augustus, called Octavian before receiving this honorific title from the Roman Senate in 27 BCE, emerged as the dominant political figure in Horace's lifetime and brought to an end a long period of civil war among the Romans. His rule also brought to an end the republican form of government, whose power lay in the Senate, the consuls, and the assemblies, and ushered in what we now call the Roman Empire, a government that was based primarily on the rule of one individual. Horace's life and work were deeply influenced by the times in which he lived.

In his later life, Horace became close to the political and intellectual elite of Rome, but he did not start out as part of that milieu. Horace was born the son of a freedman, or ex-slave. His father worked as a *coactor argentarius,* or auction agent; we do not know anything about his mother. Horace's father may have become enslaved during the so-called Social Wars (91–87 BCE), or wars with the allies, in which Horace's birthplace, the town of Venusia, which had a lesser version of citizenship called Latin rights, was taken by the Romans. When the fighting ended, Venusia was granted full Roman citizenship. Social status was very significant among the Romans, and the distinction between slave and free was a fundamental one. Horace's lower status, as the son of a freedman, may have made his rise to importance within Roman society somewhat more difficult. Roman society had a certain amount of social fluidity, but one's status always mattered.

Finances and social status, though, did not have the automatic correlation one might expect. Despite issues of status, Horace's father was wealthy enough to educate his son along with sons of the Roman elite, providing him with an education that was typical for those from families of the equestrian and senatorial classes. (Among free people three classes were distinguished: senatorial, the very wealthy who had political careers in the Senate; equestrian, the wealthy nonsenatorial class; and last, the common people. Former slaves ranked below the common people in social status, even though they might have wealth.) Horace's father brought him from his home in Venusia to the city of Rome for his early education. In Rome, Horace studied, among other authors, the early Latin writer Livius Andronicus as well as the great Greek poet Homer. He, along with other prosperous young Roman men, continued his education at an advanced level by studying philosophy at Athens, a standard place for the final stage of education. Another student at Athens during Horace's time there was the son of Marcus Tullius Cicero, the famous orator and politician.

The first century BCE had seen a lot of political upheaval in Rome. The formation of the First Triumvirate, the alliance of Pompey, Julius Caesar, and Crassus, in 60 BCE, challenged the rule of the Senate and showed that leaders backed by armed force and members of nonsenatorial classes could not be ignored. However, the alliance did not last. Crassus died. Pompey became more tied to the Senate. There were constitutional irregularities on Caesar's part and on Pompey's. The showdown came when Caesar crossed the Rubicon River in 49 BCE, which signaled his defiance of Roman law, for he was illegally leading his army across the border of the province he commanded. Thus, by the time Horace was in his teens, the former allies, Pompey and Caesar, had become engaged in a civil war. The next year Caesar defeated Pompey at the battle of Pharsalus and went on to rule Rome until his assassination. After Julius Caesar's death in 44 BCE, fighting broke out between the liberators, or tyrannicides (depending on the political perspective concerning Caesar's removal), led by Brutus and Cassius and the heirs to Caesar's power, Octavian and Mark Antony. About six months after Caesar's death, Brutus came to Athens looking for men to recruit for his side. Horace, like Cicero's son, joined the cause of those trying to keep the republic alive.

During his service in Brutus's army, Horace was appointed to the rank of military tribune, or *tribunus militum*. This rank, which conferred equestrian status upon its holder, was normally reserved for those men headed for a political career in the Senate. It was not typical for the son of a freedman, like Horace, to hold this particular rank, and Horace reports being taunted about it, showing that certain privileges of class were jealously guarded. Despite the somewhat unusual appointment in terms of his social status, it is likely from what we know that Horace had already met the financial requirements for being an equestrian even before this military appointment. Once again, despite his social circumstances, Horace managed to follow a path that was more typical for those coming from elite families. His prospects changed, though, in some ways after the battle of Philippi in 42 BCE, where Mark Antony and Octavian defeated the republican forces, in which he was included.

In the aftermath of Philippi, much land in Italy was confiscated for Octavian's victorious soldiers. When Horace returned to Italy, pardoned by the victors, he found himself without his paternal home and estate. At this point Horace writes that poverty drove him to write. We should not take this at face value because, as we will see, he was not actually poor. What his statement likely entails is an indirect comment upon his changed political fortune as well as his loss of property. These factors may have helped him choose to start along the path towards becoming a professional poet. We know that he was not poor because he was still able to purchase for himself the job of *scriba quaestorius*, clerk to the quaestors, officials in charge of the public treasury. This position involved work with public finance as well as with the public records. It was an important job, requiring both intelligence and knowledge. The position was held for life. Its great value for Horace was that it provided him with a continuous income while only intermittently demanding a great deal of his time. For a poet who wanted to be able to write, this was an ideal position. It is unlikely that Horace ever expected to be supported by his writing.

By the early thirties BCE, not long after Philippi, Horace likely was sharing his writing with others. He became friends with the famous poet Vergil, as well as the now lesser-known poet Varius. These two introduced Horace to Gaius Cilnius Maecenas, a very wealthy man of equestrian rank, whose family had originally come from Etruria, north of Rome. Nine months after this introduction, Maecenas invited Horace to become part of his circle of friends, an event that would prove central to Horace's life and work. Maecenas served as an important adviser to Octavian until the late twenties BCE, and his circle included many important poets. Thus, through his friendship with Maecenas, Horace became connected with the intellectual and political elite of his day.

Horace gave his literary friend a prominent and honored position in his writings as addressee of the first poem of his initial lyric collection (*Odes*, Books I–III) as well as the beginning poems of the *Epodes; Satires*, Book I; and *Epistles*, Book I. There is no question that Horace's relationship with Maecenas was very important to him. While some have characterized their relationship as that of patron to client, it is probably more appropriate to see Maecenas as friend and supporter. From what we can tell, Horace's relationship was not one of financial dependence, but rather one of mutual friendship and respect. Horace was employed and did not need someone to support him financially. Even though Maecenas did give Horace gifts, as friends are known to do, there is no specific evidence that Horace's Sabine farm, the country home he valued so much, was a gift from his friend.

After Philippi, Antony and Octavian held power together, but not for long. Their conflict escalated into another civil war. Antony joined forces with Cleopatra, queen of Egypt. Octavian's forces defeated them at the battle of Actium in 31 BCE. Their subsequent suicides left Octavian's power secure. Peace under Augustus came at a price. Civil war was finally over, but rule by a single leader was definitively established. Both involvement with and a somewhat detached perspective on the new Augustan order characterized Horace's life and poetry. Although connected to those with influence and power, like Augustus and Maecenas, Horace managed to maintain a certain distance. As noted above, he accepted Augustus's commission to write the *carmen saeculare*, yet he turned down a request by Augustus to serve as his personal secretary. This position would have involved helping the busy Augustus with his extensive correspondence. Horace claimed ill health, but this appears to have been just an excuse. Augustus did not hold this refusal against him, and their relationship remained cordial.

It is interesting to see that a man who did not start life as part of the

Roman elite and who had not always sided with the winning faction man-
aged to become so prominent and well regarded as a poet that he was
invited to compose a poem for a state occasion. Did he become a "court
poet" or did he maintain his independence? Like his friend and fellow poet
Vergil, Horace recognized and celebrated some of the positive changes that
Augustus brought to Rome while, in my opinion and in that of many other
scholars, maintaining a certain wariness about the price of that peace. That
a somewhat ambiguous embrace of the Augustan Age was possible under
Augustus may suggest that poetry, for a time, could hold on to a certain
kind of independent authority. Shortly after the time of Vergil and Hor-
ace, the poet Ovid was exiled by Augustus. For Horace and Vergil, though,
Rome managed briefly to be a cause for celebration but also for sober re-
flection. Whether in Vergil's work or in Horace's, one hears the voice of a
generation that experienced civil war and its losses and wondered about the
fate of a society that would become dependent on a single man's rule. Just
as Horace started off socially as something of an outsider, as a mature poet,
he tried to maintain a kind of independence, keeping a voice that, through
poetry, attempted to encompass even the authority of the state. By celebrat-
ing Rome, Horace became larger than Rome.

## Horace's Writings

Horace wrote poetry over a period of about thirty years. He is probably
best known today as the author of the *Odes,* the *Satires,* and the *Ars Poetica.*
Since the present volume is a translation of the *Odes,* that work will be dis-
cussed at greatest length. Some knowledge of his other work, however, will
be useful for the reader of the *Odes* so that its context within his literary
output can be appreciated.

Horace's first foray into writing was in the genre of satire. Satire, or
*satura,* was first classified as a literary genre by the Romans. It consists of
verse on a variety of topics written in a conversational style from an indi-
vidual perspective. Horace's satires, also called *Sermones,* or Conversations,
are written in dactylic hexameter, the same meter used for Greek and Latin
epic poetry. They touch on a wide range of literary, social, and ethical issues
and include attacks on various human faults and frailties. Horace's *Satires,*
which consist of eighteen poems, are written in the tradition of Lucilius
(second century BCE), whom Horace calls the founder of the genre. Hor-
ace greatly admired Lucilius but attempted to write in what he considered a
more polished style. After Horace's time, Persius and Juvenal continued
the genre, writing in the first and the first to second centuries CE, respec-
tively. Horace's first publication was Book I of the *Satires.* He was thirty
years old at the time. Five years later he published Book II.

Horace's *Epodes*, or *Iambi*, like the *Satires*, were written early in his career. They consist of seventeen poems composed in dactylic or iambic meter, using for the most part epodic couplets. These couplets consist of a line of one metrical structure and length followed by another of a different length and sometimes a different metrical structure. The *Epodes* follow in the literary tradition of the early Greek poet Archilochus, (seventh century BCE), who wrote poems of attack and blame. While stating that his meters and spirit come from his model, Horace tells us that his words and subject matter do not. The *Epodes* contain a number of poems on erotic topics as well as several involving politics. Although the *Epodes* on technical grounds can be called *lyric*, this term is often used only to refer to Horace's *Odes*. Stylistically, the *Epodes* fall somewhere between the more informal, conversational style of the *Satires* and the "song" of lyric.

Before we turn to the *Odes*, a few words should be said about the rest of Horace's poetic oeuvre. In 17 BCE Horace utilized lyric meter in the commissioned *carmen saeculare*. He returned to dactylic hexameter, the meter used for the *Satires* early in his career, for the writing of the *Epistles* in his later years. The *Epistles* consist of twenty-three verse essays (Book I has twenty, Book II has three), written in the form of letters. They address a variety of topics, many of them literary or philosophical in nature. *Epistles* II.3, better known as the *Ars Poetica*, includes discussion of the problems of literary composition. It has gained a place among major influential writings of literary criticism.

In 23 BCE Horace published a collection of lyric poetry, the *Odes*, or *Carmina*. It consisted of three "books" of poems. Ten years later he returned to lyric and produced a fourth book of *Odes*. The 103 poems of the *Odes* (88 in Books I–III and 15 in Book IV) are pieces that form a collection. There is an overall structure as well as a developmental, or progressive, pattern from ode to ode within the original collection, published in 23 BCE. Structural patterns exist in Book IV as well. While each ode may be read individually, reading the *Odes* as a whole has a certain cumulative effect. Repetitions, recollections, and variations within the lyrics strengthen their impact.

The term *ode* comes from the Greek word for "song," while *carmina* is the plural of *carmen*, the Latin word for "song" or "poem." Although *lyric* poetry originally referred to poetry written to the accompaniment of the lyre, Horace's lyrics, it is generally agreed, were spoken and not sung. When Horace alludes to "song" in his lyrics, he is likely doing so as a gesture towards the history of the genre. In antiquity, lyric poetry was further defined as poetry written in the meters used by the Greek lyric poets: Alcaeus, Sappho, Anacreon, Alcman, Stesichorus, Ibycus, Simonides, Pindar, and Bacchylides. Although Catullus, writing a generation earlier than

Horace, wrote some Latin poems in lyric meters (e.g., Poem LI, his transla-
tion or adaptation of Sappho Poem XXXI), Horace prided himself on hav-
ing been the first to do so on a grand scale. The variety of meters used in
the *Odes* is something Horace makes a point of displaying. Each of the first
nine odes of Book I is written in a different meter, which showcases this
accomplishment right from the start.

The notion of literary originality for the Greeks and Romans meant
something different from what one might expect from a contemporary
perspective. Rather than looking to write something completely different
from what had been written in the past (if that were even possible), classical
authors, to a greater extent than would be true of today's authors, viewed
themselves as writing within a tradition that would give generic shape to
their work. From within the parameters of those genres, originality would
be found. Rather than avoiding influence from the past, writers like Horace
thrived on it and announced it with pride. Influence is present in a wide
variety of ways. On a number of occasions, Horace takes a short passage
from earlier writers as a jumping off point for a poem, thus making his
connection with earlier literary traditions at the same time he is staking out
new literary territory for himself. Although Horace mentions Catullus only
once by name in his poetry (*Satires* I.10.19) and not at all in the *Odes*, his
influence is apparent. In fact, Horace calls attention to his connection with
Sappho via Catullus by reworking Catullus's own echo of Sappho in his
*Odes* I.22. 23–24: *dulce ridentem . . . dulce loquentem* (sweetly laughing . . .
sweetly speaking). To mention another example, in *Odes* I.37, which cele-
brates the defeat of Antony and Cleopatra at the Battle of Actium in 31 BCE
and Cleopatra's subsequent suicide, Horace begins with an imitation in the
same meter of a fragment from the Greek poet Alcaeus about the death of
the tyrant Myrsilus. Thus, while writing about a central event in contem-
porary Roman history, Horace ties himself to an earlier literary tradition
and set of historical events. This feature of Horace's style, the incorpora-
tion of a piece of earlier literature for use in his new context, is particularly
interesting in light of the fact that his *Odes* have, in turn, become a major
source for excerpting for later writers and cultural figures. (See on "carpe
diem" below.)

Horace's *Odes* show influence from many writers, both Greek and
Roman. Two of the Greek lyric poets to whom Horace especially looked for
inspiration were Sappho and Alcaeus, who lived and wrote on the island
of Lesbos, in Aeolia, the Greek area of Asia Minor, at the close of the sev-
enth century BCE. He frames his first lyric collection (Books I–III) with
poems containing references to these poets. In *Odes* I.1, which opens the
collection, Horace speaks of the "Lesbian lyre," *Lesboum . . . barbiton,* while

in the closing poem, *Odes* III.30, he speaks of "Aeolic song," *Aeolium carmen*. More specifically, in *Odes* III.30 he refers to himself as having been *princeps*, "the first or leading one," to have adapted Aeolic song to Italian poetry. The juxtaposition of the Greek Aeolic with the Latin *carmen* is noteworthy as an enactment of Horace's accomplishment. Horace took pride in having taken a genre already developed in Greek literature and bringing it to the Latin language and to Rome. Like Catullus, Horace was influenced by the Alexandrian aesthetics of Callimachus (third century BCE), the Hellenistic Greek poet who described his Muse as "slender," a term that Horace utilizes in reference to his own Muse as well. The notion of the slender Muse involved valuing the small, learned, carefully wrought poem. While Horace does venture at times towards a grander style, for example, like that of the Greek poet Pindar, the majority of his poems display a more restrained manner.

Most of the odes are addressed to a particular individual, real or fictitious (we do not always know which). This puts into place a formal structure of speaker and addressee. Some of the addressees are connected in obvious ways to the poems; at other times their connections remain more elusive, particularly if we, as modern readers, do not know the identity of the addressee, or even whether he or she is "real" or "fictional." The variety of addressees in the *Odes* is indicative of the blending of Greek and Roman, personal and political, imaginary and contemporary, within the poems. Such varied figures as Maecenas, Augustus, Vergil, Agrippa, Sestius, Aristius Fuscus, Pyrrha, Leuconoe, Lydia, Thaliarchus, and even an unnamed *puer* (boy / [young] male slave / male beloved) serve as addressees. They show that the world of the *Odes* is both "real" and "literary." These poems reflect the diversity of "Horace's world," and attempts to sort out the realities from the fictions within the lyrics are not necessarily worthwhile. Boundaries between Rome and Greece, literature and "reality," seem to be intentionally blurred.

While Horace was writing self-consciously in a long literary tradition that included much Greek influence, his poems are very contemporary as well. They reflect in many ways the world of first century BCE Rome in all of its social and political complexity. While Roman matrons may be chastised for adultery in one of the Roman *Odes* (III.6), elsewhere freer sexual and social relations for men with socially indeterminate or less "reputable" (and therefore more accessible) partners (male or female) may be presented as attractive (see, e.g., *Odes* I.23, II.8, or IV.1). Horace's was a world in which some women were gaining greater independence, but that did not mean there was no concern over the behavior of upper-class women. Five years after Books I–III of the *Odes* were published, Augustus passed his first set of laws regulating marriage and adultery. Horace's use of non-Roman names for many of the figures who function as objects of desire in the *Odes* has the effect of locating desire at a safe remove from Roman freeborn citizens. For example, in *Odes* I.5, the famous ode to Pyrrha, we encounter an attractive and dangerous woman: Is she to be viewed as a Greek courtesan living in Rome? a freedwoman? an imaginary figure?

The *Odes*, with their mix of literary tradition and contemporary sensibility, range widely in subject matter, including such topics as poetics, morality, philosophy, politics, Rome, time, death, the erotic, banquets, and friendship. However, they are not easy to categorize by topic because they blend various themes and shift emphases along the way. Poems that begin with one theme may end with another. The development of the individual ode is sometimes surprising, starting in one place and ending in another. For example, *Odes* I.4 begins with the loosening of spring from winter and ends with the figure of Lycidas, a shifting male object of desire, who will be lost to the addressee upon his death but will continue for the living as the object of male and, later, female desire. While the seasons and death and love are all related in the poem, the shifts along the way force the reader away from thinking that the poem can be "about" any one of these things alone. Although the odes include what one might characterize as philosophical moralizing with elements of Epicureanism (and some of Stoicism) included, it is delivered in such a way as never to be mere lecturing. The injunction to enjoy life is set more broadly in the awareness of life's brevity. The sympotic impulse is grounded in an awareness of impending death. Categories like the personal and the public often overlap. Public events lead to private celebrations. Philosophical teaching blends with erotic strategies. Ironic detachment at times belies passion. Still further, Horace incorporates even topics he says are beyond the scope of lyric, thus expanding the genre's possibilities. To give an example, in *Odes* I.6, while refusing to write epic, the grand genre beyond the scope of smaller lyric, Horace brings epic description into his lyric. Therefore to say what the *Odes* "are about" is almost impossible. They seem to be about whatever Horace chooses, even about the very things that he announces are beyond their scope.

Horace adapts his "slender" genre not only to embrace wide subject matter but also to maintain the power of the poet in changing times. Just as Vergil's *Aeneid*, Rome's "national epic," combines praise of and anxiety about the new Roman order in the heroic, yet flawed, figure of Aeneas, so the *Odes* are fully engaged with the new Augustan rule yet maintain a certain separation from it. In *Odes* I.37, for example, mentioned above for its use of a beginning based on Alcaeus, celebration of Octavian/Augustus's defeat of Antony and Cleopatra ends with a noble picture of Cleopatra, the enemy, because through her suicide she avoids the degradation of appearing in a Roman triumph. The final line of the poem describes Cleopatra in praiseworthy fashion as a *non humilis mulier* (a not humble woman), and the final word of the poem, which follows this phrase directly, is *triumpho* (triumph). The odes of Book IV, which include several in praise of Augustus or his family (see, e.g., Odes 2, 4, 5, 14, and 15), are still the work of a poet who manages to retain some kind of independence from the Augustan regime. They are not Augustan propaganda, but rather poems that take seriously the world of politics while reasserting the power of poetry. In *Odes* III.30, though, it is significant that Horace proclaims that his work will live on and even grow in reputation while the pontifex climbs the Capitolium with the Vestal Virgin. This almost conditional statement contextualizes Horace's representation of his work, for it joins his fame to Rome's sacred center and its state religion. (The Capitoline gods, Jupiter, Juno, and Minerva, were worshipped on the Capitoline hill, and the *pontifex maximus,* or chief priest, and the Vestal Virgins, guardians of Rome's sacred flame, represent officials charged with maintaining Rome's religion and its rituals.) In hindsight Horace's words show rather poignantly the lasting power of poetry over the temporary vagaries of Roman rule and its symbolic religious rituals, for, of course, Horace's reputation has exceeded the temporal limit for it that he indirectly suggests it might have.

There is a protean quality to the *Odes*. What appears on the surface is often undermined. What glimmers in one light may shift in another. Horace is a master of litotes and indirection. (Litotes involves understatement, usually through the assertion of something by denying its opposite.) Recall the words about Cleopatra, above: a *not humble* woman. Horace often assumes a distanced pose, which leaves somewhat ambiguous his relationship to his material. Given these characteristics, it may seem paradoxical that he became known as a source of familiar philosophical wisdom in the form of mottoes or catchphrases. Horace is easily quotable, but the sense of these phrases, pulled out of context, may be distorted, incomplete, or at least less nuanced. Particular quotations, taken from Horace's *Odes* and popularized, show both Horace's fame and his characteristic elusiveness. In the three examples that follow, we will see how returning these phrases to their original context provides both a richer understanding of the quotable phrases and a sense of what can be lost when fragments of poetry are taken from the specificity of their context.

Horace is likely best known today as the author of the phrase *carpe diem* (seize the day). The English poets Andrew Marvell and Robert Herrick employed the carpe diem motif, which entails the idea of taking advantage of the present because tomorrow is unknown. Byron was apparently the first to actually use the Latin phrase in English in a letter of 1817, which was published in 1830 by Thomas Moore: "I never anticipate,—carpe diem—the past at least is one's own, which is one reason for making sure of the present."[1] Our popular culture has since absorbed the phrase, bringing it into common use. For example, it appears as the name of a 2002 limited-edition watch produced by Rado in collaboration with the Swiss graphic designer Karl Gerstner. Specifically, each second the dial of this watch changes its colors and forms, calling attention to every passing moment. Carpe diem is also the new motto of the NBA basketball superstar Kobe Bryant, whose new (actually revived) jersey number 24 reflects the theme of hard work 24/7. (Bryant wore the number 24 in the early part of his high school career.) A limited-edition signed basketball, complete with Latin motto, has been produced. Still further, moviegoers have heard the phrase in a much-quoted line from the film *Dead Poets Society* (1989),[2] delivered by Keating, the inspiring English teacher, to his students about how to live one's life: "Carpe, carpe diem, seize the day, boys, make your lives extraordinary." This line follows upon the teacher's attempt to elicit the meaning in Herrick's "Gather ye rosebuds while ye may . . ." (from "To the Virgins, to Make Much of Time") and to make it relevant to his students' lives.

Horace now reaches many who likely do not even know they know a Horatian phrase. This not only suggests that the *Odes* are a repository of easily quotable material but also points out the temptation to pull Horace's words out of context and the sometimes disruptive result. While the English poets mentioned above both continue and elaborate upon the theme present in the original Horatian context, those who know the phrase *carpe diem* only from popular culture may be surprised when they see it in its original context. Not just an isolated philosophical admonition about the present, the phrase occurs in a poem that has a particular speaker addressing a particular addressee. The phrase comes from the final line of *Odes* I.11:

. . . carpe diem, quam minimum credula postero.

The whole sentence reads:

. . . dum loquimur, fugerit invida
aetas: carpe diem, quam minimum credula postero.
(lines 7–8)

1. *Letters and Journals of Lord Byron: With Notices of His Life* (Paris, 1830), 251.
2. Written by Tom Shulman and directed by Peter Weir.

Here is my translation:

> While we are speaking, jealous time will have fled: seize [or, more literally, "pluck"] the day, trusting as little as possible in the next [one].

The speaker and his addressee are talking. Time is jealous. Despite the generalizing potential of the now-famous phrase, the addressee's hoped-for positive response to the speaker's utterance, "seize the day," serves to benefit the speaker of the poem, as teacher and/or potential lover, and the phrase is embedded in the speaker's philosophical and/or amatory designs. Still further, the "next (one)" is typically taken to mean the next "day." However, an ambiguity created by the absence of an expressed noun that the adjective *postero* (next) would modify leaves the door open for the interpretation "next man." This creates an alternative, more self-interested, version for what may seem like just selfless, dispassionate advice. Is it time (the next day) that shouldn't be trusted or the next man (as opposed to the present/speaking one)? Of course, the personification of time as "jealous" helps to suggest this less conventional, but perhaps more interesting, interpretation. Horace cleverly becomes both the wise man offering sage comments on how to live life and the indirectly desiring speaker who devises the appropriate rhetorical strategy for gaining what he wants.

We have seen that the phrase *carpe diem* becomes more complicated, and perhaps more interesting, when read in its original context. There are other Horatian phrases, too, that have reached a wide public in a form that may leave forgotten their original context. For example, the phrase "golden mean," *aurea mediocritas,* which comes from *Odes* II.10, taken out of context, might suggest the valuing of the exact middle between two extremes. The phrase in English, according to R. G. M. Nisbet and Margaret Hubbard,[3] is first attested in 1587. The reader, though, who knows the philosophical background to the poem, including Aristotle's remarks in the Nicomachean Ethics,[4] will realize that the "mean" of ideal behavior, from this perspective, does not necessarily fall in the exact middle between extremes. The Latin word *mediocritas* carries a sense of "moderation" that the English word *mean* limits too much. Part of what makes the poem interesting is its avoidance of simple maxims. For example, rather than saying "You will live properly, if . . ." Horace begins his poem with a comparative adverb *rectius,* which means "*more* properly." Thus, the advice given is not guidance for the perfect life, but rather wisdom to guide the reader

---

3. *A Commentary on Horace Odes Book II* (Oxford: Oxford University Press, 1978), 160, citing F. P. Wilson, *Oxford Dictionary of English Proverbs,* 3rd ed. (Oxford: Clarendon Press, 1970).
    4. 1106$^{a}$27 ff.

merely to a "better" life. The use of comparatives continues—and Horace uses these to great effect throughout the *Odes*—when a huge pine tree is seen as disturbed "more often" by the winds (than a smaller one would be), and the lofty towers fall down with a "heavier" fall. Just as the carpe diem injunction becomes more complex and perhaps more interesting when seen in its original Horatian context, so too, the notion of the golden mean, or moderation, in the context of the ode, becomes much fuller. Life is not black and white. Seemingly simple advice embedded in its poetic context takes on a sophistication not apparent in the disembodied phrase.

A final example of the Horatian phrase and the importance of its original context can be found in Wilfred Owen's famous World War I antiwar poem, "Dulce et Decorum Est." Much of the bleak power of the poem comes from Owen's prefacing his concluding quotation from the Latin of Horace "dulce et decorum est pro patria mori" (it is sweet and appropriate to die for one's country) with his own English words, "The old Lie," which undercut and comment upon it. The reader of Horace, though, will know the Horatian lines in the source that come *after* Owen's brief quotation. They move beyond the statement of the value of dying for one's country to the statement that the soldier who runs away in battle ends up dying too. Obviously, examining the full Horatian context (*Odes* III.2.13–16) puts a slightly different light on the idea of the value of patriotism, since we see that in Horace death comes to valorous soldier and coward alike.

We can recognize that the *Odes* appear to be eminently quotable. Bold statements, phrases, and ideas stand out from these poems. The Horatian phrase, especially delivered in Latin, has a kind of grandeur to it. Yet the reader of Horace will understand that there is far more to the *Odes* than these quotable phrases. When reinserted into their original context, they have much more to offer, or perhaps, something different to offer the reader than he or she might have anticipated. The reader who becomes familiar with the *Odes* will see how a disembodied quotation can unravel much of what Horace is about.

The German philosopher and classicist Friedrich Nietzsche, in a now very famous statement, described the effectiveness of Horace's lyrics as a "mosaic of words, in which every unit spreads its power to the left and to the right over the whole, by its sound, by its place in the sentence, and by its meaning."[5] There are few descriptions of Horace's *Odes* that could better capture the power of Horace's words and his skill at choosing them and arranging them. Horace is considered a first-rate craftsman of the Latin

5. *The Complete Works of Friedrich Nietzsche*, vol. 16, *The Twilight of the Idols*, ed. Oscar Levy, trans. Anthony Ludovici (London, 1927), 113.

language. He is known as much for how he writes as for what he writes. The *Odes* are concise. Each word in them carries much weight.

Stunning, self-conscious word placement is one of Horace's greatest poetic feats. Word order, it should be noted, in Latin is quite flexible because of the language's inflected nature. In inflected languages words show their function in a sentence, not through the order of the words, as in English, a positional language, but through word transformations. In Latin, this typically means a change in the word's ending. For example, *mulier* is the subject form of the Latin word for "woman," while *mulierem* is the direct object form. Where the given form of the word is placed in the sentence, that is, beginning, middle, or end, has no effect on its grammatical function. For example, **Mulierem** *videt vir* and *Vir* **mulierem** *videt* and *Vir videt* **mulierem** all mean "The man sees the woman." because *mulierem* is the direct object form each time and *vir* is the subject form. In English, of course, word order is essential for determining grammatical function. "The man sees the *woman*." means something different from "The *woman* sees the man." Because of these differences, therefore, the Latin poet automatically has more choice about what position to place words in than the poet writing in English, but Horace exploits the poetic possibilities of word order more than almost any other Latin poet.

Two specific features of Horace's style that relate to Latin word order and exemplify the tessellated quality of his lyrics noted by Nietzsche are his use of hyperbaton and of *callida iunctura*. (Hyperbaton is a rhetorical figure involving the radical displacement of words from their normal word order.) An example of this device can be seen in the Cleopatra ode, mentioned above. The adjective *superbo* (proud/arrogant) is the last word in the poem's penultimate line. The noun this adjective modifies is *triumpho* (triumph), the poem's final word in the final line.

> privata deduci superbo
>   non humilis mulier triumpho.
> (*Odes* I.37, 31–32)

They are divided by three other words, *non humilis mulier*. This use of hyperbaton—here, the wide separation of adjective and noun it modifies—has a number of effects. It leaves temporarily open-ended what or who is being described as "proud" or "arrogant." It also juxtaposes *superbo* (proud/arrogant) with its not-quite-synonym *non humilis* (not humble). While once the idea is completed at the conclusion of the poem one realizes that it is Augustus's military triumphal procession (*triumpho*) which the adjective *superbo* (proud/arrogant) modifies, the intervening words about Cleopatra and the litotes of "not humble" make the word hover around the figure of Cleopatra. Finally, despite the grammatical agreement of *superbo* and *triumpho*, the distance of the adjective from its noun leaves the noun somewhat apart, and one could argue that the notion of the triumph in some sense attaches itself to the *non humilis mulier* through the power of word order. This is the sort of rhetorical power that is not uncommon in the *Odes*. In this instance, a somewhat ambivalent stance towards even the great figures and events of the day is promulgated through the literary device of hyperbaton.

*Callida iunctura* (clever joining) is a phrase that comes from Horace's own *Ars Poetica* (*Epistles* II.3.47–48). It refers to the making new of familiar vocabulary through careful juxtaposition. It is another device, like hyperbaton, that takes advantage of Latin's flexible word order. Horace's vocabulary in the *Odes* is fairly prosaic. The newness that he brings to words is often derived from their placement next to other words that then color their sense, rather than through the introduction of unusual vocabulary. For example, Pyrrha, the object of desire in *Odes* I.5, is described as *simplex munditiis* (simple [in her] refinement/elegance). The juxtaposition of *simplex* and *munditiis* creates a slightly paradoxical phrase—to what extent can one be both "simple" and "refined"? Can guilelessness and artfulness be combined? Art and artifice, trust and deception, are central to this ode, as the reader will see. The juxtaposition of these two words is one way in which Horace images the tension that is Pyrrha.

While in some sense language is always linear, moving forward in time and space, it clearly functions in others ways as well. When reading Horace's *Odes*, we need to read and reread in order to see some of the sophisticated poetic techniques that give Horace's lyrics the mosaic quality Nietzsche named so well.

## Translation

The pontifex and Vestal Virgin are gone (or at least radically transformed), but one can still climb the Capitolium, or Campidoglio, as we would say today in Italian. Visitors to Rome regularly see that old ruins are intertwined with modern structures. An English translation of Horace's *Odes* in some sense resembles the Rome of today—pieces of the past mingled with pieces of the present, old language with new. As someone who has been attracted to Horace's poetry very much for its sound and style in Latin, I have rarely found pleasure in reading it in English translation. Jeffrey H. Kaimowitz's translation of the *Odes* has changed that. He manages to capture the rhythmic feel—the speed and cadence—of Horace's phrases and sentences, keeping their elegance and grandeur. This volume manages to stay true to both the sense and the aesthetic pleasure of the poetry—no easy task. When I read Kaimowitz's *Odes*, I can still hear Horace's voice.

The Odes of Horace

# BOOK I

---

## I.1

Maecénas descended of ancient kings,
oh you my sweet adornment and support,
there are some men who pleasure find to swirl
Olympic dust in chariots, avoiding
turn posts with swift wheels: earthly lords,
the far-famed palm transports them to the gods;
another's happy if Rome's fickle mob
contends to raise him to the consulship;
another, if within his granary
he gathers all the wheat of Africa.
The man who loves to hoe his father's fields
you'd not dislodge with royal promises
to play the frightened sailor plowing through
Aegean waters with a wooden ship.
The merchant fearing winds in combat with
the Sea of Ícarus[1] will praise his town's
repose and countryside, but soon repairs
his shattered craft, untaught to live with little.
There is the man who does not scorn a cup
of fine old wine or hours of leisure in
the day, now stretched beneath a leafy tree,
now by the waters of a gentle spring.
For many, army life's the choice and sounds
of horns combined with bugle blasts, and wars
abhorred by mothers. Under freezing sky
the hunter waits, forgetting his young wife,
if his faithful dogs have seen a doe,
or if a boar breaks through the woven nets.
As for myself, ivy, prize of poets,
mingles me with gods on high, the sacred
grove and nimble dance of nymphs with satyrs

*First Asclepiad system*
1. The eastern Aegean.

part me from the crowd, if Eutérpe
grants her flutes and Polyhýmnia[2]
obliges tuning the Aeólic lyre.
But if you include me with the lyric
bards,[3] with head held high I'll touch the stars.

2. Euterpe (well-pleasing) and Polyhymnia (she of many songs of praise), both
Muses.
3. A reference to the nine canonical Greek lyric poets: Alcman, Sappho, Alcaeus,
Stesichorus, Ibycus, Anacreon, Simonides, Pindar, and Bacchylides.

I.2

Now enough ill-omened snow and hail has
Jove, our father, poured on earth and, hurling
with right hand aglow against our sacred
       citadel,[1] frightened

Rome, frightened nations lest the painful
times that Pyrrha[2] mourned return, the
strange events, when Proteus[3] forced his seals to
       visit high mountains

and the fish clung fast to the elm's top branches,
which had been the dwelling of the doves, while
fearful deer were swimming mid the inun-
       dating flood currents.

We beheld the yellow Tiber madly
twisting back his waters from the Tuscan
shore to topple Numa's palace and the
       temple of Vesta,[4]

while the spreading river played avenger
for his very much aggrieved wife Ília,[5]

---

*Sapphic stanza*
1. The Capitoline Hill has two summits, one the site of the arx (citadel), the other
the location of the temple of Iuppiter Optimus Maximus (Jupiter the best and great-
est), the holiest temple in Rome. N-H (18–19) argue that the flood referred to in the
poem may be the one that occurred on 16–17 January 27 BCE.
2. Pyrrha and her husband, Deucalion, through the warning of his father, Pro-
metheus, built a boat and survived a flood sent by Zeus (= Jupiter) to punish the
wickedness of mankind.
3. A minor sea god, responsible for herding seals.
4. Both the temple of Vesta, with its sacred hearth tended by the Vestal Virgins,
and the adjacent Regia, the so-called Palace of Numa (the second king of Rome)
and headquarters of the *pontifex maximus* (chief priest) and his fellow priests, were
located in the Roman Forum.
5. Ilia, daughter of the king of Alba Longa, after giving birth to Romulus, future
founder of Rome, and his twin, Remus, was thrown by her usurping uncle, along
with the boys, into the river Tiber. The Tiber river god, in Horace's version of the
story, then took Ilia as his wife, and the twins were washed ashore and suckled
by a wolf. Ilia's name connects her with Aeneas and his son Ilus, founder of Alba
Longa, and thus with Julius Caesar and Augustus, who traced their lineage back to
Aeneas and Ilus.

flowing past his eastern bank, against
    Jupiter's wishes.

Youth now thinned in ranks will hear that citizens
had sharpened steel by which harsh Persians
better had been slain, will hear of strife from
    their parents' failings.[6]

Which god should the people call upon to
save the crumbling state? With what words should the
holy virgins[7] plead to Vesta, now less
    open to prayers?

Whom will Jove assign to expiate our
sin? We pray that you at last may come,
mantling your bright shoulders with a cloud,
    augur Apollo;

or if willing, you, smiling Venus Ery-
cína,[8] round whom Mirth and Cupid flit or
you, ancestor Mars, if you care for your
    line and descendants,

you, alas, too sated by long sport, whom
crys and glinting helmets gratify and
Marsian[9] soldiers fiercely glaring at their
    blood-stained opponents;

or winged Mercury, if you with altered
form adopt a young man's features[10] here on
earth, allowing yourself to be called
    avenger of Caesar,[11]

---

6. A reference to the intermittent civil wars, from 49 to 31 BCE.

7. Vestal Virgins, members of the sole major female priesthood in Rome, who tended the never-to-be-extinguished fire in the temple of Vesta.

8. Eryx, on the west coast of Sicily, was the site of an ancient temple of Venus.

9. Tribe of central Italy whose fierce soldiers served in the Roman legions.

10. Augustus.

11. Caesar here refers to Julius Caesar, who in his will adopted as his son and heir his grandnephew Octavius, who henceforth was known as Gaius Julius Caesar Octavianus (later to receive the honorary title *Augustus*).

late may you return to heaven and long
may you happy dwell among the Roman
people, nor turned hostile by our failings
    may swift winds carry

you away, but here enjoy great triumphs
and the name of Father and First Citizen,[12]
nor let the Persians ride unpunished,
    while you rule, Caesar.

12. *First Citizen* (Latin *princeps*) was a republican title used by Augustus in the constitutional arrangement he created "of restoring the Republic."

## I.3

May Venus, who on Cyprus rules,[1]
   may Helen's pair of brothers, shining stars,[2]
and Aéolus, who rules the winds,
   with all in check except for Iapyx's blowing,[3]

guide you straight, o ship, who hold
   my Vergil[4] in your trust: from Attic shores,
I pray, that you may bring him safely
   back, and so save half of my own soul.

That man had oak and triple bronze
   about his heart who first commended to
the savage sea his fragile craft,
   and took no fear in struggles of the winds

nor in the dismal Hýades[5]
   nor in the raging southern gale, lord of
the Adriatic as none else
   in raising up and putting down the swells.

What tread of death could he have feared
   who with dry eyes beheld within the deep
its monsters, who saw the wild waves
   and ill-famed cliffs—Acroceraúnia?[6]

*Fourth Asclepiad system*
This is a *propempticon*, a poem wishing a prosperous journey.
   1. Venus (= Aphrodite), born of the sea foam (Greek *aphros*), was a regarded as a
patron of seafaring.
   2. The Dioscuri, the brothers of Helen, Castor and Pollux, are patron gods of
sailors and conceived as appearing to those in need in the phenomenon of Saint
Elmo's fire, which is a faintly luminous discharge of electricity observable as a flam-
ing phenomenon on ships' mastheads during a storm.
   3. Iapyx, the west-northwest wind, favored the crossing from Brundisium on the
southeast coast of Italy to the west coast of Greece.
   4. Horace's good friend, the poet Vergil (70–19 BCE).
   5. Group of stars in the constellation Taurus, whose "morning setting (Novem-
ber) and evening rising (late October) were supposed to indicate rain" (N-H, 50–51).
   6. A prominent landmark—"Highlands of Thunderstorms"—on the west coast
of Greece that Vergil would see on his voyage.

God in vain with foresight split
   the land from ocean incompatible,
if nonetheless ships go against
   his law and leap across forbidden shoals.

Daring to go through anything,
   the human race speeds on without restraint.
Daring Prométheus[7] carried down
   to mankind fire, using foul deceit;

when fire was purloined from heaven's
   heights, an undreamt host of wasting ills,
descended hard upon the earth
   and death, which cannot be escaped, before

slow-footed, quickened its step.
   The empty air was tried by Daédalus[8]
on wings not natural to man,
   and Hercules broke through the way to Hell.[9]

Nothing's too much for men who die:
   we even seek in folly heaven's heights
and through our evil won't allow
   an angered Jove to stay his thunderbolts.

7. The divine figure stole fire from the gods and gave it to mankind, thus initiating human technological development.

8. The master craftsman created wings made of feathers and wax to escape imprisonment on Crete.

9. As the last of his twelve labors, Hercules stole the guardian dog Cerberus from Hades.

I.4

Loosened is raw winter in the pleasing change of spring and
    the Zephyr: winches haul dry keels to water;
cattle care no longer for the stable nor the plowman
    his fire nor are meadows white with hoar-frost.

Venus of Cýthera[1] now leads dances under looming
    moonlight and Nymphs, hands joined to lovely Graces,
shake the earth with rhythmic steps, while fiery Vulcan
    surveys the Cýclopes' imposing workshops.[2]

Now it's time to bind anointed hair with fresh, green myrtle
    or flowers which the earth, released, can offer.
Now in groves it's time to sacrifice to Faunus[3]
    a lamb or kid, whichever one he wishes.

Pale impartial Death pounds doors of poor men's hovels
    and kingly towers. Wealthy Séstius,[4]
life's brief span forbids us to enter hope far-reaching;
    soon night will press upon you and the Manës[5]

and the meager house of Hades; once you pass there,
    you'll not be playing games at drinking parties,
nor admire young Lýcidas,[6] who kindles passion
    in all the lads and soon will warm young women.

*Change*

*Third Archilochian system*
1. Traditional birth place of Venus, an island off the southeast coast of the Pelo-
ponnese in the south of Greece.
2. The one-eyed giants created Jupiter's thunderbolts overseen by Vulcan, god of
the forge and husband of Venus.
3. A Roman god of the forests and protector of flocks identified with the Greek
god Pan.
4. Lucius Sestius, a man of republican sentiments, respected by Augustus, who
appointed him suffect consul in 23 BCE.
5. Spirits of the dead.
6. An evocative male name borrowed from Greek pastoral poetry.

## I.5

What slight young man awash with fragrant scents
pursues you, Pyrrha,[1] on a rosy bed
    within a charming cave? For
        whom is your blond hair tied back

in simple elegance? Alas, how often broken
faith and fickle gods he'll mourn and be
    amazed at seas turned hostile
        by black squalls! The innocent,

he now enjoys you, thinks you are like gold,
expects you always lovely and avail-
    able, unaware of
        treach'rous gusts. Wretched those

for whom you gleam untried: I too, as
the votive tablet on the temple wall
    makes known, hung up to Neptune[2]
        clothing dripping from the storm.

*Third Asclepiad system*
    1. From the Greek word for fire (pur); N-H comment (74) that "the name sug-
gests a girl with reddish-yellow or auburn hair."
    2. The Latin actually has *potenti . . . maris deo,* (to the potent divinity of the
sea), which is usually interpreted as Neptune; some, like N-H following Zielinski
(79–80), against the evidence of all the manuscripts, read *deae* (to the goddess),
which is interpreted as Venus (= Aphrodite) born of the sea foam (Greek *aphros*).
Quinn (132) suggests with Horace's "sedulous avoidance of the obvious point" that
"to the potent divinity of the sea" could apply to a generalized "divinity." This could
include Neptune or Venus or both.

## I.6

You'll be described by Várius[1] the epic
bard as brave and conqueror of the foe,
whatever forces fierce on sea or land
    achieve at your command.

Agríppa,[2] we do not attempt to tell
of this or of Achilles' unrelenting spleen
or sly Ulysses' travels on the deep
    or Pelops' savage line,

huge themes where we are small: modesty ╰
and a muse strong in warless song forbid
us to diminish splendid Caesar's praise
    or yours through want of skill.

Who will in worthy fashion write of Mars
arrayed in bronze, Meríones begrimed
with Trojan dust or Diomédes[3] godlike
    through Minerva's aid?

We sing of parties, sing of fights by maidens
keen with sharpened nails against young men,
we who are free or if we're scorched by love,
    lightly as usual.

*Second Asclepiad system*
    1. Varius Rufus was a well-respected contemporary poet, who, along with Vergil,
introduced Horace to Maecenas.
    2. Close friend and leading general of Augustus, Marcus Vipsanius Agrippa
(ca. 63–12 BCE) was crucially involved in the defeat of Mark Antony and Cleopatra
at the climactic battle of Actium in 31 BCE.
    3. Meriones and Diomedes were Greek heroes of the Trojan War.

I.7

Some will glorify Mytiléne or shining Rhodes or
  Ephesus or the walls and double
harbor of Corinth or Thebes renowned for Bacchus or Delphi
  famed for Apollo or Thessaly's Tempë;[1]

others' single-minded purpose is the praise of
  chaste Athena's city in endless
verses, to wear on their foreheads the common sprig of olive;
  many will, to honor Juno,

tell of Argos that nurtures horses and wealthy Mycenae;
  as for me, not steadfast Sparta
nor Larísa's fertile plain has such attraction
  as Albúnea's[2] thundering grotto

and the headlong Ánio[3] and the grove of Tibúrnus[4] and
  orchards watered by swift moving brooklets.
As the South Wind, often clearing, sweeps clouds from the
  darkened sky and does not bring forth

rain continuously, so you remember to wisely
  limit grief and life's distress with
mellow vintage, Plancus,[5] whether in an army
  camp agleam with standards or some day

in your Tibur's dense shade. When Teucer[6] departed his father
  and his Sálamis, exiled, he still is

*First Archilochian system*
1. All famous sites in Greece.
2. The sibyl (prophetess) of Tibur, a resort town northeast of Rome on the Anio.
3. The modern river Aniene, which separates Sabine country from Latium,
where Rome is located; at Tibur it descends in a series of falls.
4. A traditional founder of Tibur, near which Horace had his Sabine farm.
5. Lucius Munatius Plancus, said to be a native of Tibur, was an agile politician
who survived the civil wars.
6. Teucer and his half-brother Ajax were both sons of Telamon of the island Sala-
mis near Athens. When Teucer returned to Greece after the Trojan War, Telamon
blamed him for the death of Ajax at Troy and banished him. Teucer then sailed to
Cyprus, where he founded a new city named Salamis.

said to have bound on his temples, while drinking, a garland of
    poplar,[7]
speaking thus to grieving friends:

"Wherever Fortune kinder than my father brings us,
    we will go, my companions and comrades.
You should not despair with Teucer to lead and guide you,
    for unerring Apollo has promised that

"in a new land there'll be a rival Sálamis. Brave
    heroes, you have often suffered
worse with me: now with wine dispel your cares—tomorrow
    we will plough again the vast sea."

---

7. N-H (104–5) note that poplar has a special connection to Hercules, "the patron
of adventurers and explorers," and, like Hercules, "Teucer is perhaps given a poplar
crown because he is going on a dangerous journey."

## I.8

Lydia,[1] say, by all the
    gods, I beg you, why you hasten Sýbaris[2] through love to
ruin, why he shuns the
    sunny Field of Mars,[3] he who bore dust and heat. Why does

he not ride among his
    cavalry companions nor with iron bit control his
Gallic steed? Why is
    he afraid to touch the yellow Tiber? Why does he

avoid anointing[4] more
    cautiously than poison nor display arms bruised from exercise,
who often with the
    javelin and discus was renowned for setting records?

Why does he lie hidden,
    as they say the son of Thetis[5] did before the woeful
deaths at Troy, that manly
    dress not drag him into bloodshed with the Lycian forces?[6]

*Greater Sapphic system*
1. A name redolent of luxury and pleasure.
2. Sybaris, the city, was famed for its soft and pleasure-seeking way of life.
3. *Campus Martius* in Latin, the Tiber flood plain on the northwest side of Rome, which, during the republic, was used as an exercise ground, meeting area, and voting place, but gradually was built up, especially during the empire.
4. Anointing with olive oil was an integral feature of ancient athletics.
5. Thetis, mother of Achilles, hid him on the island of Scyros dressed as a girl at the court of King Lycomedes to prevent his fated death at Troy.
6. Allies of the Trojans.

I.9

Do you see how Sorácte[1] stands clothed white
in layers of snow and struggling boughs sustain
    their load no longer, while from piercing
        cold the rivers have stopped flowing?

Dissolve the winter weather, put more logs
upon the fire, and more generously
    pour from the Sabine bottle[2] that wine,
        Thaliárchus,[3] aged for four years.

Allow the gods the rest, for once they've stilled
the winds contending on the boiling sea,
    the cypresses are not shaken
        nor the ancient manna-ash trees.

Of what will be tomorrow, do not ask:
whatever days that Luck provides account
    as gain, and, while a youth, don't spurn the
        sweet delights of love and dancing,

as long as you are green, not peevish with
gray hair. Seek now once more the Field of Mars,
    the plazas, and soft whispering towards
        nightfall at the time appointed,

seek now what gives away a hidden girl,
her pleasing laughter from a secret place,
    and tokens snatched away from arms or
        fingers but barely resisting.

*Alcaic Stanza*
    1. A mountain (2,400 ft.) about twenty miles north of Rome and visible from the city.
    2. A wine originating in the area near Horace's farm and not an expensive vintage.
    3. Greek name meaning "initiator / in charge of good cheer."

I.10

Mercury, well-spoken grandson of Atlas,[1]
you who shrewdly shaped the savage ways of
early men through speech and seemly training
    in the palaéstra,[2]

you I celebrate the messenger of
great Jove and the gods and parent of the
lyre, skilled at hiding what you please in
    humorous thieving.

You were just a baby, when lord Apollo
sternly threatened if his cattle you removed
by guile were not returned, yet laughed,
    deprived of his quiver.

And with you to lead him, wealthy Priam,[3]
going out from Ílion,[4] eluded
Atreus' haughty sons,[5] Thessalian fires,[6]
    all that was hostile.

You establish righteous souls in blissful
habitation and with golden wand
control the throng of shades, to gods on high and
    gods below welcome.

*Sapphic stanza*
1. His mother was Maia, daughter of Atlas.
2. Mercury (= Hermes), versatile and mischievous, was the patron god of ora-
tory and literature as well as of athletics. The palaestra was a wrestling school and a
symbol of athletics in general.
3. King of Troy.
4. On his way to ransom the body of his son Hector from his slayer Achilles, as
described in *Iliad* XXIV.332 ff.
5. Agamemnon and Menelaus, leaders of the Greek forces against Troy.
6. I.e., guards at the camp of Achilles, who was from Phthia in Thessaly.

I.11

Don't ask, you cannot know, what end for me or you
the gods have set, Leucónoë.[1] Don't look into
the stars. Much better to submit to what will be,
whether Jove bestows more winters or makes this
the last which pummels now the Tuscan sea against
a rocky shore. Be wise, decant your wine, prune back
long growth of hope. As we speak, begrudging time
has fled. Seize the day—and trust tomorrow least.

*Fifth Asclepiad system*
1. This name, apparently from the Greek words *leukos* (white) and *nous* (mind),
has been thought by some to mean something like "simple" or "naïve."

I.12

What man or what hero do you choose to
praise with lyre or shrill flute, Clio?[1]
What god? Whose name will playful Echo
    cause to resound

along the shady slopes of Hélicon or
by the Pindus, or on icy Haemus,[2]
whence the forests rashly followed singer
    Orpheus, who through the

music that his mother[3] taught him checked the
rapid course of rivers and swift-rushing
winds and charmed the oaks to go with him, when
    hearing his sweet strings?

What should I declare before accustomed
praise of father Jove, who rules affairs of
men and gods, who orders in their seasons
    sea, land, and heaven?

Out of him arises nothing greater
than himself and none in strength is like him
or his second. Pallas[4] nonetheless is
    nearest in honors,

bold in battle. Nor in silence, Liber,[5]
will I pass you by nor you, Diana,[6]

*Sapphic stanza*
1. This Muse's name appears to derive from the Greek word *kleiein* (to celebrate).
2. Helicon is a mountain in Boeotia in central Greece, the Pindus a mountain
range in central Greece dividing Epirus from Thessaly, and the Haemus a moun-
tain range in Thrace in northern Greece.
3. Usually identified as the Muse Calliope.
4. Another name for the Greek goddess Athena, usually identified with the
Roman goddess Minerva.
5. Roman god of fertility and wine, identified with Dionysus/Bacchus, god of
wine, intoxication, and ecstasy.
6. Roman goddess identified with Artemis, Greek goddess of woodlands and
wild nature and usually represented as a huntress. Artemis was the twin sister of
Apollo.

hostile to fierce beasts nor you, Apollo,
  feared for sure arrows.

I will tell of Hercules and also
Leda's sons,[7] one famed for horsemanship, the
other for his fists, whose star, when once its
  glowing light's flashed to

sailors, water pounding on the rocks recedes, the
winds diminish and the clouds are scattered,
and the threatening waves subside within the
  sea, as they've ordered.

After these, first should I mention Romulus
or Numa's quiet kingdom or the
haughty Tarquin's[8] power or the heroic
  death of Cato?[9]

Gratefully I'll tell in noble song of
Régulus,[10] the Scauri, and of Paulus
bravely dying on the field of Cannae,
  and of Fabrícius.

Stringent poverty and his ancestral
farm with household gods brought forth that man as
well as rough-hewn Cúrius, skilled in war, and
  also Camíllus.

Like a tree, as time proceeds, Marcéllus'[11]
fame is growing; mid them all the Julian

---

7. The Dioscuri, Castor and Pollux, renowned respectively as a horseman and a boxer and protectors of sailors; the "shining star" is probably a reference to Saint Elmo's fire, identified with the Dioscuri (see Ode I.3).

8. Romulus, Numa, and Tarquin, first, second, and final king of Rome.

9. Marcus Porcius Cato (95–46 BCE), a firm Stoic and stubborn hero of the late republic (see Ode II.1). The next two stanzas present a series of military heroes from the early republic.

10. See Ode III.5.

11. Interpreted by some to be Marcus Claudius Marcellus, a great hero of the Second Punic War. Others identify another Marcus Claudius Marcellus, son of Gaius Marcellus and Octavia, sister of Augustus, who, married to the emperor's daughter Julia, was intended as his successor but died prematurely, in 23 BCE.

family's star[12] shines bright, as does the moon
   among lesser fires.

Father and protector of the human
race,[13] born of Saturn, in your care is
placed great Caesar's fate: with Caesar your
   lieutenant, may you reign.

Whether he'll parade in rightful triumph
conquered Parthians[14] who threaten Latium[15]
or the Indians and Chinese near to
   the Eastern Ocean,[16]

under you, he'll rule the wide world justly:
you will shake Olympus with your chariot,
you'll hurl thunderbolts opposed to groves that
   are pure no longer.[17]

12. A reference to the family of Caesar Augustus, who had been adopted in Julius
Caesar's will as son and heir.

13. Jupiter.

14. The Parthian dynasty, the Arsacids, ruled from the Euphrates to the Indus
from 247 BCE to 224 CE, and their most effective forces were horse archers.

15. The territory in which Rome is located.

16. The Romans at this time had a hazy knowledge of east Asia and believed the
Pacific was much closer to the Mediterranean than it was.

17. N-H note (168–69) that Augustus was especially devoted to Jupiter the Thun-
derer (Iuppiter Tonans), who was supposed to strike with lightning only sacred
groves that had become polluted.

I.13

Whenever, Lydia, you praise
    the wax smooth arms of Télephus,[1] the rosy
neck of Télephus, ah,
    my seething liver swells with aching bile.

Then neither my complexion nor
    my mind remain in balance; furtive tears
slip down my cheeks, attesting to
    how utterly I'm ravaged by slow fires.

I smolder if excessive rows,
    brought on by wine, put blemish on your fair
white shoulders, or the ardent lad
    has bruised upon your lips a telltale mark.

If you would hear me closely, you
    would not expect that always he will wildly
wound that lovely mouth of yours,
    which Venus steeped in nectar's finest part.

O three times blest and more are they
    whom fast a bond unbroken holds as one,
whom love not rent by ugly strife
    will not release before their final day.

*Fourth Asclepiad system*
    1. N-R in their commentary on Book III (238) say that "the name Telephus may
have suggested 'shining far,'" from the Greek words *tēle* (far) and *phōs* (light).

I.14

O ship, new waves will carry you to sea
again. Why hesitate? Bravely head
  for port. Don't you see one
    side is stripped of all its oars,

your mast and yardarms, wounded by the swift
South Wind, are groaning and your hull without
  its undergirding set of
    ropes can scarcely stand against

the too commanding sea? No sails intact,
no gods upon the stern to call for help
  once more, though Pontic pine,[1] a
    child of a forest famed,

you boast your name and lineage uselessly:
the timid sailor has no faith in painted
  ships. Unless you owe the
    winds a cause for sport, beware!

Not long ago you were my weary worry:
now my heart's desire and deep concern,
  avoid the waters flowing
    round the gleaming Cýcladës.[2]

*Third Asclepiad system*
  This poem takes its inspiration from a poem of Alcaeus, and the Roman rhetori-
cian Quintilian regarded it as an allegory with the ship representing the state. What
events it refers to are not easy to pin down. Another possibility is that the ship rep-
resents a former lover for whom Horace expresses continuing anxiety.
  1. Pontus, a region in northern Asia Minor, was famed for its timber used in
shipbuilding.
  2. The group of islands in the central Aegean.

I.15

When faithless Paris carried off by sea
his host's wife Helen on Idaéan[1] galleys,
Nereus[2] stilled the swift winds with unwelcome
    calm that he might sing

harsh fate: "With evil omen you lead home
one whom with many soldiers Greece will seek
returned, sworn to smash your marriage and
    the ancient realm of Priam.

"Alas, what toil horse and hero face,
how many deaths you bring upon your people.
Now Pallas[3] is preparing helm and aegis,
    chariot and rage.

"In vain emboldened through the aid of Venus,
you will comb your hair and to the warless
lyre trill songs pleasing to the ladies,[4]
    in vain with marriage bed

"you will avoid stout spears and Cretan arrows,
battle's din, and Ajax swift in your
pursuit: alas though late, you still will foul
    your wanton locks with dust.

"Do you not notice at your back Läértes'
son,[5] your people's doom, and Pylian Nestor?

Second Asclepiad system
    1. Ida was a mountain range near Troy, from which presumably the wood was
cut to build the ships that Paris used to carry off Helen of Sparta and thus start the
Trojan War. While a shepherd on Ida, he won this "privilege" by judging Venus the
most beautiful in a contest with Juno and Minerva.
    2. Nereus was a sea god, and like other sea gods, he had the gift of prophecy.
    3. Pallas Athena (= Minerva), who sided with the Greeks, is usually represented
with a helmet and with the aegis, a goat skin with a Gorgon's head in the middle
and fringed with snakes, worn over the breast.
    4. See *Iliad* III.380 ff.
    5. Odysseus.

Sálamine Teucer[6] and Sthénelus, skilled
   in war or, if there's need

"to handle horses, keen charioteer,
press you intrepidly. Meríones
you'll also know. Look: fierce Diomédes
   rages after you,

"whom you, just like a stag that's seen a wolf
across a valley, heedless of herbage,
will flee, soft creature, panting hard—not this
   you promised to your love.

"The anger of Achilles will postpone
the day for Ílion and the Trojan women:
after a fixed sum of winters pass,
   Greek flames will burn Troy down."

6. See Ode I.7.

I.16

O daughter fairer than her mother fair,
you'll put whatever end you wish to my
    reproachful iambs,[1] be the means by
    flames or stormy Adriatic.

Not Cýbele, not Liber, not Pýthian
Apollo derange the minds of priests
    within their shrines as much, the córybants[2] do
    not clash cymbals with such fervor,

as sullen anger, which neither savage fire
nor Nórican steel[3] nor shipwrecking seas
    nor Jupiter himself descending
    in a thunderbolt deters.

Prométheus, we are told, constrained to add
a little plucked from every quarter to
    the primal clay, set within our
    hearts the frenzied lion's fury.

Anger flung Thyéstes[4] down in grim
destruction and has been the reason why
    proud, lofty cities perished utterly
    and a disdainful army

pressed deep into the walls a hostile plough.[5]
Restrain your passion. Heat of feeling in

*Alcaic stanza*
1. Beginning with the Greek poet Archilochus, whom Horace imitated in his
*Epodes*, verse in iambic meter was often a vehicle of abuse.
2. Youthful orgiastic worshipers usually associated with Cybele, the great mother-
goddess of Phrygia.
3. Noricum encompassed eastern Alpine lands south of the Danube and was val-
ued by the Romans for its iron deposits.
4. The sons of Pelops, Thyestes and Atreus, were bitterly at odds—Thyestes
because he did not receive the throne of Mycenae, Atreus because Thyestes
seduced his wife. This of course was the beginning of a series of crimes through
the generations of the family, ending with the killing of Aegisthus, son of Thyestes,
by Orestes, grandson of Atreus.
5. When a city was destroyed, its remains were often then ploughed over.

> sweet youth afflicted me as well and
>     sent me off to hasty iambs,
>
> enraged: now I seek to trade the sullen
> for the gentle way, as long as you
>     in turn, when I've recanted my
>         abuse, become my friend and love me.

I.17

Swift-footed Faunus[1] often changes Mount
Lycaéus[2] for agreeable Lucré-
   tilis[3] and keeps from my she-goats
      rain-filled winds and fiery summer.

In safety through protected woods the harem
of the smelly husband wanders off
   in search of thyme and scarce arbutus
      nor do kid-goats fear green serpents

nor wolves, who are the favorites of Mars,
whenever, Týndaris,[4] the valleys and
   smooth rocks of sloped Ustíca[5] have
      resounded with the sweet-toned panpipe.

The gods protect me, my devotion and
my muse are pleasing to the gods. Here
   for you will flow abundance from the
      horn that spills the country's splendors.

Here in a deep-set valley you'll avoid
the Dog Star's heat and to a Tean lyre[6]
   describe Penelope and dazzling
      Circe longing both for one man.[7]

Here under shade you'll quaff the harmless wine
of Lesbos,[8] nor will Bacchus son of Sémele,

*Alcaic stanza*
   1. A Roman god of the forests and protector of flocks, identified with the Greek
god Pan.
   2. A mountain in western Arcadia in the Greek Peloponnese, associated with Pan.
   3. A mountain in the Sabine country near to the country villa of Horace.
   4. A name with perhaps Arcadian associations, though the woman herself is no
shepherdess.
   5. Another mountain in Sabine country.
   6. In the appealing manner of the lyric poet Anacreon of Teos.
   7. Both his wife, Penelope, and the sorceress Circe loved the hero Odysseus.
   8. Lesbian wine was reputed most pleasing and not apt to cause drunkenness.
The reference could also be to the enjoyment of Horace's poetry, which was
strongly influenced by the the poets of Lesbos, Sappho and Alcaeus.

along with Mars, bring on battles
    nor, suspected, will you fear that

hotheaded Cyrus[9] will inflict his reckless
    hands on you, who are no match, and tear
        the garland clinging to your tresses
        and your unoffending clothing.

9. N-H (226) comment that "the name seems to belong to Hellenistic erotic verse." The Greek word *kuros* (= Latin *cyrus*) means "supreme power, authority" and may be significant in the context of the poem.

I.18

Plant no tree, Varus,[1] prior to the sacred vine
round Tibur's gentle land and Cátilus's[2] walls.
For God has promised hardship to non-drinkers nor
will gnawing apprehension otherwise depart.
After wine, who prates of war or poverty?
Who rather would not speak of you, lord Bacchus, and
of you, fair Venus? Lest one trespass temperate Liber's[3]
rites, the Centaurs' boozing battle with the Lapiths[4]
stands a warning as is Eúhius stern to the
Sithónians,[5] when, lustful, they divided right
from wrong by but a sliver. Brilliant Bássareus,
I'll not rouse you unwilling nor disclose to light
your frond-wrapped emblems.[6] Check the savage tambourines
and Berecýntic flutes,[7] which bring on blind self-love
and vainglory that lifts too high its empty head
and faithlessness betraying secrets clear as glass.

*Fifth Asclepiad system*
1. Identified in one group of manuscripts as the friend of Horace, the critic Quin-
tilius Varus, subject of Ode I.24, but perhaps more plausibly scholars have identi-
fied the distinguished jurist and consul suffect in 39 BCE, Publius Alfenus Varus.
2 . A legendary founder of Tibur, a resort town northeast of Rome on the Anio
River.
3. In addition to Bacchus, in the poem Horace refers to Dionysus with his Latin
name *Liber* and his Greek orgiastic titles *Euhius* and *Bassareus.*
4. At the wedding of Hippodamia and Pirithous, king of the Lapiths, the Cen-
taurs, who were among the invited guests, attempted to carry off the women,
including the bride.
5. A Thracian tribe.
6. Dionysus's sacred emblems, known only to initiates of Bacchic rites.
7. The Berecyntes were a Phrygian tribe, so the adjective is poetic for "Phrygian."
These flutes were originally associated with the goddess Cybele, who originated in
Phrygia.

I.19

The ruthless Mother of Desires,[1]
  with the Theban son of Sémele,[2]
and lustful Wantonness demand
  I yield again, though I've forsaken love.

The gleam of Glýcera,[3] who shines
  more brightly than the whitest marble, scorches
me, her pleasing brazenness
  and face too ravishing to look upon.

Rushing against me, Venus has
  deserted Cyprus nor permits me speak
of Scythians or Parthians attacking
  in retreat[4] and things that matter not.

Here put for me an altar of
  fresh turf, here put green sprigs and incense with
a cup of unmixed wine:[5] for with
  a sacrifice, more gently she will come.

*Fourth Asclepiad system*

1. Venus.

2. Dionysus, god of wine, whose mother was Semele, daughter of Cadmus, king of Thebes, and whose father was Zeus (= Jupiter).

3. The name means "sweet woman" and was often used by courtesans.

4. A favorite tactic of the Parthian horsemen was to turn while fleeing and let fly arrows at their pursuers.

5. Incense and wine, not diluted with water, were integral preliminaries to a sacrifice. The usual practice for Greeks and Romans at meals and parties was to mix their wine with water.

I.20

You shall drink from modest bowls cheap Sabine
wine which I myself stored sealed within a
Grecian jar[1] the time you were applauded
    so in the theater,[2]

splendid knight Maecénas,[3] your paternal
Tiber's banks,[4] together with the playful
echoing Mount Vatican,[5] resounded
    loud with your praises.

You may drink at home choice Caécuban and
fine wines pressed at Calës: no Falérnian
vineyards nor the hills of Fórmiae make
    mild my goblets.[6]

*Sapphic stanza*

1. Greek jars were sealed with a cork smeared with pitch.

2. Maecenas was applauded in the theater of Pompey after recovering from a serious illness.

3. Maecenas, though descended of Etruscan royalty, never chose to follow an aristocratic political career as a senator, preferring to remain through his wealth an *eques* (knight), a member of Rome's next highest social class.

4. N-H (249) observe that "the Tiber, like Maecenas, came from Etruria" and "that the river rose in the *territorium* of Arezzo, Maecenas's home town."

5. N-H note (250) that "the echo would naturally come from the long line of the Gianicolo, which is directly opposite on the other side of the Tiber, and not from the modern Vatican, which is too far north." They point out that in antiquity the whole area was called *ager Vaticanus* (Vatican territory).

6. All four wines named in this stanza are premium vintages, Caecuban and Formian being from Latium, close to Rome, and Calenian and Falernian from Campania, nearer Naples.

I.21

Speak of Diana, maidens young and fair,
speak, lads, of the long-haired Cýnthian,[1]
    and of Latóna[2] held in
        deep esteem by sovereign Jove.

Extol her[3] who delights in streams and groves
conspicuous on icy Álgidus[4]
    or in the forests of green
        Gragus[5] or black Erymánthus.[6]

You, young men, extol with equal praise
the Vale of Tempe[7] and Apollo's birth-
    place, Delos, and his shoulder
        for his lyre and quiver famed.

He from our people and great Caesar, he
will turn grim hunger, plague and grievous war
    against the Persians and the
        Britons, prompted by your prayers.

---

*Third Asclepiad system*

1. Cynthian (= Apollo), born with his sister twin Artemis (= Diana) near Cynthus, the one hill on the Aegean island of Delos.

2. Mother by Jupiter of Diana and Apollo.

3. Diana.

4. Mountain in the Alban Hills near Rome, the first of three mountainous locations mentioned in the stanza that are or could be associated with Diana as the goddess of wild nature.

5. Mountainous area in Lycia in southwest Asia Minor.

6. Mountain in the wilds of Arcadia in the center of the Greek Peloponnese.

7. Beautiful valley, associated with Apollo, in northeast Greece, between Thessaly and Macedonia.

I.22

One who's pure in life and free of evil
has no need of Moorish spears nor bow nor
of a quiver, Fuscus,[1] loaded full of
    poisonous arrows,

whether he should journey by the seething
Syrtes[2] or amid the uninviting
Caucasus or through the realms washed by the
    storied Hydáspes.[3]

For a wolf within the Sabine woodland,
while I sang of Lálagë[4] and wandered
off without a care beyond my boundary,
    fled me defenseless—

such a monster as is not reared in the
warlike land of Daunus[5] with its broad oak
forests nor is bred in Juba's kingdom,[6]
    parched nurse of lions.

Put me on the barren northern steppes, where
no tree stands refreshed by summer breezes,

*Sapphic stanza*
    1. Aristius Fuscus was a schoolmaster, a lover of city life, and a good friend of
Horace who refused to extricate the poet from his comic predicament with an
annoying admirer in Horace's Satire I.9, "The Bore."
    2. Dangerous shoals along the coast of North Africa between Carthage and
Cyrene, which today are in Tunisia and Libya, respectively.
    3. River Jhelum in Pakistan's Punjab region, where Alexander the Great in 326
BCE defeated the Indian king Porus.
    4. The name means "prattler."
    5. Northern Apulia in southern Italy, where Horace's native city, Venusia, was
located. Daunus was a mythical king of the region.
    6. Juba II (d. ca. 23 CE) was ruler of the north African kingdom of Mauretania,
which encompassed modern-day Morocco and western Algeria.

that division of the world that clouds and
    ugly skies trouble,

put me where the sun above is much too
near, a place denied to habitation:
I will cherish sweetly laughing Lálagë,
    sweetly prattling.

I.23

You shun me, Chloë,[1] very like a fawn
that seeks her fearful mother over pathless
    hills, not without a
        needless fear of wind and woods:

for if with spring's arrival leaves have rustled
in the trees or grass-green lizards pushed
    aside the bramble bushes,
        her knees tremble, her heart thumps.

And yet not like a savage tigress or
a Moorish lion I chase after you.
    Stop chasing after mother:
        you are ready for a man.

*Third Asclepiad system*
   1. The name means "the first green shoot of plants" in spring and suggests fresh-
ness and immaturity.

I.24

What shame or limit should there be to grief
for one so dear? Teach a mournful song,
Melpómene,[1] whom Jove has favored with
    a clear voice and the lyre.

Now endless sleep holds our Quintílius.[2]
When will Modesty and Justice's sister,
uncorrupted Faith, and naked Truth
    ever find his like?

For many men his death's a cause for tears,
for no one more than you, Vergílius.[3]
In vain, alas, you beg the gods, whom you
    have trusted, to free him.

But why? If more beautifully than Thracian
Orpheus you play strings that charm the trees,
would blood come back into his lifeless shade,
    which Mercury, not kind

to prayers that death's gates be unlocked, has driven
with his dreadful staff to Hades' throngs?
It's hard, but patience will make lighter what's
    forbidden to be changed. *patience*

*Second Asclepiad system*
1. A Muse whose name means "songstress."
2. The critic Quintilius Varus, a good friend of the poet.
3. The poet Vergil.

I.25

Much less often brazen fellows shake your
shuttered windows with a rain of pebbles
nor do they disturb your sleep; the door
    embraces the threshold,

which before would open on such easy
hinges. Less and less you hear now: "Are you
sleeping, Lydia,[1] while I, your love, must
    suffer through long nights."

It is your turn to lament the scorn of
libertines, despised in lonely alleys,
while the Thracian wind,[2] when there's no moon, runs
    riot in revels.

Burning lechery and fiery passion,
which can drive the broodmares to a frenzy,
will be raging round your ravaged liver,[3]
    not without complaint

that exuberant young manhood finds more
joy in fresh green ivy and dark myrtle,
withered leaves it offers to the East Wind,
    winter's companion.

*Sapphic stanza*
1. A lady with the same voluptuous name appears in Odes I.8 and 13.
2. N-H note (297) that Thrace, home of the winds for the Greeks, "was always
the Siberia of the ancients."
3. Seen by the ancients as the seat of sexual desire.

I.26

The Muses' friend, I'll hand my sadness and
my fears to reckless winds to carry to
    the Cretan sea, without a care at
        all what king of icy regions

is feared up north or what intimidates
prince Tiridátes.[1] You who take delight
    in pristine fountains, weave bright flowers,
        weave my Lámia[2] a garland,

sweet Muse of Pipla.[3] Lacking you, praise I
confer is useless. It is fitting that
    you and your sisters honor him with
        new song and Aeólic measures.[4]

*Alcaic stanza*
1. A pretender to the throne of Parthia during the early years of the reign of
Augustus.
2. N-H (301) suggest that this is Lucius Aelius Lamia, a contemporary of Horace
and a successful general in Spain in 24 BCE.
3. Pipla, near Mount Olympus in southeast Macedonia, was identified with the
Muses.
4. Verse in the style of Sappho and Alcaeus, and the poem is, fittingly, in Alcaic
stanzas.

I.27

To fight with cups created to bring joy
is Thracian.¹ Do away with barbarous
    behavior and defend from bloody
        altercations modest Bacchus.

How monstrously a Persian scimitar
conflicts with wine and candlelight: my friends,
    calm this irreligious² clamor
        and remain upon your couches.

You wish that I as well partake of dry
Falérnian? Let Opúntian
    Megýlla's³ brother tell by what wound
        blessed he perishes, by what shaft.

Not inclined? On any other terms
I will not drink. Whatever love subdues
    you, burns with fires not a cause for
        shame, and you are always falling

for someone who's respectable. Come, tell
us who it is: our ears are safe. You wretch,
    poor boy deserving of a better
        love, you struggle with Charýbdis.⁴

What witch, what wizard with Thessalian drugs,⁵
what god can ever disentangle you?
    Winged Pégasus will scarcely set you
        free, bound fast by this Chimaéra.⁶

*Alcaic stanza*
    1. The Thracians, a people on the northern border of Greece, were considered
primitive and prone to heavy drinking.
    2. Because it offends Bacchus.
    3. An exotic Greek location, Opuntian Locris in central Greece, and an exotic
Greek personal name provide a Hellenistic setting.
    4. A deadly whirlpool, identified as being in the Straits of Messina between Italy
and Sicily and a symbol of rapacity, especially that of courtesans.
    5. Thessaly was well known for witches and potent herbs and potions.
    6. The monster, with the head of a lion, body of a goat, and tail of a snake, was
slain by Bellerophon riding the winged horse Pegasus.

I.28

Measurer of the sea and land and of the sands that
    lack a number, Archýtas,¹ a little
tribute of some dust confines you by the Matine²
    shore nor does it profit any

to have probed the airy mansions and explored the
    heaven's round vault with mind that must perish.
Even Tántalus has died, the guest of the gods, and
    also Tithónus, though carried to the

heavens,³ and Minos, knowing Jove's secrets, and Tartarus holds
    Pythagoras dispatched again to
Hades, though he, lifting down Euphórbus's shield and
    taking Trojan times as witness,

yielded nothing to dark death but flesh and sinews,
    he no mean authority on
truth and nature, as you attest.⁴ But just one night and
    road to trod but once await all.

Furies make some a spectacle in Mars' grim arena,
    greedy seas bring an end to travelers:
crowded are the mingled funerals of old and young:
    Prosérpina⁵ cruelly misses no one.

I too was overwhelmed on the Adriatic by the
    raging South Wind in stormy November.

*First Archilochian system*
1. A leading Pythagorean philosopher and mathematician of the fourth century
BCE and a native of Tarentum.
2. An unidentified geographic location in southern Italy, perhaps near Tarentum.
3. Tithonus was loved by Aurora (Dawn), who obtained for him immortality but
crucially neglected to secure him eternal youth, so that he eventually shriveled away
to almost nothing.
4. Pythagoras believed he was a reincarnation of the Trojan hero Euphorbus and,
to substantiate his claim, in the Argive Heraeum correctly identified a shield as
belonging to Euphorbus.
5. The Latin form of the Greek goddess of the dead and wife of Hades, Perse-
phone.

But you, traveler, don't begrudge the kindness of a
    little bit of shifting sand to

cover my unburied bones; this done, whatever
    on Italian seas the East Wind
threatens, may the forests of Venúsia be scourged, while
    you continue safe, and may much

recompense be yours from guardian Neptune and favoring
    Jove. Do
    you ignore you do a wrong that
later will harm your innocent descendants? Perhaps such
    arrogance and lack of justice

will await you too. I'll not be left with my prayers
    unavenged. No offering will free you.
Though you hasten, the delay is not long: you may
    throw three handfuls of dust[6] and rush on.

6. Ritually this would be enough.

I.29

O Íccius,[1] do you envy now as blest
the wealth of Araby, do you prepare
    a sharp campaign against the never
        humbled kings of Saba[2] and for

the fiercesome Medes[3] weave chains? What foreign maiden,
her intended slain, will do your bidding,
    what royal page, once taught to stretch his
        father's bow with Chinese arrows,

now graced with scented hair, will be assigned
to pour your wine? Who'd deny that plunging
    streams could flow back up steep mountains
        or the Tiber travel backwards,

when you would trade the school of Socrates
and books of famed Panaétius,[4] collected
    with such toil, for Spanish
        breastplates,[5] you who promised better?

*Alcaic stanza*
1. A young friend of Horace, who also appears in Epistle I.12.
2. Located in the southwest of the Arabian Peninsula, modern Yemen.
3. An Iranian people.
4. A leading Stoic philosopher of the second century BCE.
5. Even in antiquity Spain was famous for its metalwork.

I.30

Venus, queen of Cnidus, queen of Paphus,[1]
leave your favored Cyprus and pass over
to the handsome shrine of Glýcera,[2] who
    calls with much incense.

With you may the fiery boy,[3] the Graces[4]
loosening their cinctures, and the Nymphs and
Youth, unlovely lacking you, along with
    Mercury, hasten!

*Sapphic stanza*
    1. Cnidus, on the southwest coast of Asia Minor, and Paphus, on the southwest
coast of Cyprus, were sites of major shrines of Venus.
    2. The name means "sweet woman"; a Glycera appears as well in Odes I.19, I.33,
and III.19.
    3. Cupid, son of Venus.
    4. The three minor goddesses, the Graces, arm in arm, personified charm, grace,
and beauty and were represented as dancing naked.

I.31

What does a bard require of recently
enshrined Apollo?[1] With an offering of
   new wine what does he pray for? Not for
      lush Sardinia's rich harvests

nor sweltering Calabria's fine herds
of cattle, not the gold and ivory
   of India nor farms the silent
      Liris[2] laps with quiet currents.

Let those whom fortune has assigned the vines
of Calës[3] prune them, let the wealthy merchant
   from his golden goblets drain the
      wine he's bought with eastern commerce—

dear to the gods, three and four times in
a year he sails Atlantic waters with
   impunity. My olives nourish
      me, light chicory, and mallow.

Apollo, grant that I enjoy in health
the things I have and sound of mind, I pray,  X
   I not endure an old age that is
      base or lacking in the lyre.

*Stoic*

*Alcaic stanza*
1. The temple of Apollo dedicated by Augustus on the Palatine Hill on 9 October
28 BCE in gratitude for his victories over Pompey the Great's son, Sextus, in 36
BCE and over Antony and Cleopatra in 31 BCE.
2. A river in central Italy (today called the Liri in its upper portions and the
Garigliano farther down) flowing south and west from the Apeninnes and empty-
ing in the Tyrrhenian Sea.
3. A city north of Naples in the famous Campania wine-growing region.

I.32

We entreat, if ever in our leisure
we have trifled something with you that may
last this year and more, come sing my Latin
    verses, O lyre.

You were first played by the man from Lesbos,[1]
who, though brave in warfare, still, be he in
arms or if along the shore he'd moored his
    tempest-tossed vessel,

used to sing of Bacchus and the Muses
and of Venus and her child Cupid
and of Lycus[2] who with his dark eyes and
    tresses was comely.

O adornment of Apollo, tortoise
shell made lyre,[3] welcome at the feasts of
Jove, sweet, healing consolation, greet when
    duly I call you.

*Sapphic stanza*
1. The Aeolic poet Alcaeus.
2. A name redolent of Asian sensuality. No preserved poetry of Alcaeus deals
with homoerotic love, but Cicero mentions his writing on the subject.
3. The tortoise shell was used in the manufacture of the body of the lyre.

## I.33

Tibúllus,[1] do not grieve, obsessed with unkind
Glýcera,[2] or drone sad elegies,
asking why she's broken faith and now
  prefers a younger man.

Her love for Cyrus[3] burns Lycóris,[4] fair
of brow, while Cyrus favors Phóloë[5]
the harsh; but roe-deer will lie down
  with hungry wolves before

an ugly lover beckons Phóloë.
Thus Venus has decreed, whose pleasure is
to bend to her bronze yoke forms and hearts
  that do not match—cruel joke.

Although a better love was seeking me,
with pleasing bonds freedwoman Mýrtalë[6]
possessed me, fiercer than the Adriatic
  curving Calabria's coast.

*Second Asclepiad system*
  1. The Latin original actually has the name *Albius*, which without much hesitation has usually been identified with the elegiac poet Albius Tibullus (d. 19 BCE).
  2. Glycera (sweet woman) is attended by the oxymoronic adjective *immitis* (unkind).
  3. See Ode I.17.
  4. *Lycoris* was the name the elegiac poet Gallus gave his mistress, the actress Cytheris.
  5. Pholoe appears in Ode II.5, Tibullus's Elegy I.8, and Statius's Silva II.3 as the name of a girl reluctant to be loved.
  6.. *Myrtale* (Myrtle) is often found in inscriptions as the name of freedwomen.

I.34

The gods' infrequent, frugal votary,
while still I was astray, an expert in
 a mad philosophy,[1] I now am
  forced to set sail in reverse and

retrace my course. For Jupiter, who
usually divides the clouds with flashing fire,
 across a clear sky drove his flying
  chariot and thundering horses;

at this the sluggish earth and wandering streams,
the Styx and horrid seats of hated Hell
 and Atlas[2] at the limit of the
  world were shaken. God can change what

is high for low and lessens greatness, bringing
on obscurity: winged Fortune, grasping
 swiftly, plucks the crown from one and
  loves to set it on another.

*Alcaic stanza*
 1. The reference is to Epicureanism, which preached a totally mechanistic universe without divine intervention and supernatural phenomena.
 2. The end of the Atlas mountain range in western Morocco, the limit of the known Western world.

I.35

O goddess Fortune, ruling pleasing
Antium,[1] at hand to lift a mortal from
    the lowest reaches or by dealing
        death to overturn proud triumphs,

the needy farmer seeks you with vexed prayers
as mistress of the land, as mistress of
    the sea he seeks you who provokes
        Aegean waters with his vessel;

the savage Dacian fears you, and the Scythians
who fight as they retreat, and foreign peoples,
    city states, brave Latium,[2] royal
        mothers, and kings clad in purple,

lest you disdainfully kick down the propping
column, lest the swarming populace
    incite to arms, incite the hesitant
        to arms and smash the kingdom.

Before you always marches cruel Neces-
sity, who carries gripping spikes and dowels
    in her bronze hand nor lacking is the
        rigid clamp and lead to bind it;

Hope and rare Good Faith, enswathed in white, *accept whatever*
attend you, nor[3] refuse to follow you,
    whenever with changed garb you, hostile,
        leave the houses of the mighty

*Alcaic stanza*
1. There was a famous cult of the goddess Fortuna at Antium (modern Anzio),
on the western coast of Italy, south of Rome.
2. The home territory of the Romans.
3. Keeping *nec* with K and the manuscripts, while Peerlkamp, followed by SB,
emends *nec* (nor) to *sed* (but). As N-H point out (396–97), the word *inimica* (hostile)
"introduces the most extraordinary confusion. Up to this point Horace suggests
that the Fortuna of the family shares the disaster that befalls the man," and now,
"hostile," she leaves him flat. This very problematic passage does not yield easy
sense.

—but then the faithless rabble and the lying
whore withdraw, and, jars drained lees and all,
    his friends run off, too treacherous to
        bear in equal part the burden.

Protect our Caesar, now about to go
against the far off Britons, and our newly
    gathered swarm of youthful troops feared
        in the East and by the Red Sea.

Alas, we are ashamed of fratricidal
wounds and wickedness. Hard age, what do
    we shrink from? What's the sin we've left
        untried? Where has our youth through fear of

the gods restrained their hands? What altars have
they spared? O that upon new anvils you'd
    reforge our blunted swords for use
        against Masságetae[4] and Arabs.

4. Scythian tribe living east of the Caspian Sea.

## I.36

With incense, lyre, and a slaughtered
    calf as vowed, it pleases to appease
the gods protecting Númida[1]
    who, safely now returned from farthest Spain,

distributes many kisses to
    dear friends, to none, however, more than his
sweet Lámia, mindful that
    in their past boyhood Lámia was king

and that they came of age together.
    Lest this fair day lack its proper note,
no limit let there be to wine,
    nor rest for feet in leaping Salian steps,[2]

nor let hard-drinking Dámalis[3]
    best Bassus[4] at imbibing with one quaff,
nor let the feasts lack roses, nor
    the long-lived celery nor lily brief.

And all on Dámalis will cast
    their melting eyes, but Dámalis, more twining
round than ivy growing wild,
    will not be plucked away from her new love.

*Fourth Asclepiad system*
    1. Nothing is known of Numida except that from this poem he seems to have
been a close friend of Lamia, perhaps the son of the Lamia in Ode I.26.
    2. The priests of Mars, the Salii, dressed in armor and carried figure-eight
shields called *ancilia*. Their name derived from their leaping ritual dance (from the
verb *salio*, "to leap").
    3. The name in Greek means "heifer or young cow"; it should also be noted that
the word derives from the root word "to subdue."
    4. N-H (405) note that the name *Bassus* could refer to a real individual addressed
by Propertius in his poem I.4.1, but they also suggest that the name may have been
used because it is similar to the Bacchic name *Bassareus* (see Ode I.18) and may be
"the type-name for a heavy drinker," using as a possible example Martial's poem
VI.69.

I.37

Now we must drink, now with abandon stamp
upon the earth, now's the time, my friends,
        to deck the sacred couches of the
            gods with richly furnished banquets.[1]

Before it was not right to take the mellow
Caécuban from ancient stores, while yet
        the queen,[2] unbridled in her hopes,
            besotted by sweet fortune, along

with her polluted band of gelded gallants,
readied mad ruin for the holy
        Capitol[3] and Roman power.
            But when scarce one galley safely

escaped the flames, her frenzy abated. Caesar
turned her mind, crazed with Egyptian wine,
        to living fear, when with his ships he
            closely followed her flying

from Italy, just as a hawk pursues
the timid doves or nimble hunter chases
        down a hare amid the fields of
            snowy Thessaly—to fetter

with chains that deadly monster. But she wished
a death more noble: she was not afraid
        of swords, as women often are, nor
            swiftly sailed for hidden landfalls;

*Alcaic stanza*
    1. A Roman ritual, the *lectisternium*, where images of the gods were placed on
couches and food placed before them.
    2. Cleopatra VII (69–30 BCE), queen of Egypt and last of the Ptolemies, who was
defeated in 31 BCE at the naval battle at Actium by the forces of Caesar Octavian
(who later was to be called Augustus).
    3. Location of the temple of Iuppiter Optimus Maximus, Rome's holiest shrine.

she dared to calmly look upon her royal
city laid low in defeat and bravely
   handle scaly serpents to
      imbibe within her flesh black venom:

determined now to die, she was more fierce—
no self-abasing woman to be cruelly
   shipped to Rome and led without a
      crown in Caesar's lofty triumph.[4]

4. The traditional Roman victory parade.

I.38

Persian ostentation I disdain, lad,
garlands bound with lime bark do not please me,
put aside the search to find what places
    the late rose lingers.

To plain myrtle I prefer that you not
add a thing: not unbecoming is the
myrtle to you serving or to me
    beneath dark vines drinking.

*Sapphic stanza*

# BOOK II

---

II.1

The state's upheaval since Metéllus' time,[1]
the causes, crimes, and practices of war
 and Fortune's fancies and the leaders'
  painful friendships and their weapons

anointed with unexpiated blood—
you write a work that's full of gambles,
 Póllio,[2] and tread through fires
  lying under treach'rous ashes.

Allow the Muse of tragedy a little
respite from the stage: as soon as you
 have detailed Rome's affairs, you'll seek once
  more the theater's lofty mission,

O you, a bulwark to the grieved defendant
and the Senate searching for advice:
 the crown from your Dalmatian triumph
  has produced eternal honors.

*Alcaic stanza*
 1. Quintus Caecilius Metellus Celer was consul in 60 BCE, the year rising politi-
cian Gaius Julius Caesar, the established general and politician Gnaeus Pompeius
Magnus (Pompey), and the wealthy Marcus Licinius Crassus decided to cooperate
in an informal political alliance that is usually referred to as the First Triumvirate. It
marked the beginning of the final phase in the political deterioration that led to the
end of the Roman Republic as a viable political entity. In this stanza, Horace refers to
the problems of rivalry and civil war between participants in this alliance and to simi-
lar difficulties that characterized the Second Triumvirate, which two decades later
brought together Gaius Iulius Caesar Octavianus (Octavian, later to be the emperor
Augustus), Marcus Antonius (Mark Antony), and Marcus Aemilius Lepidus.
 2. Gaius Asinius Pollio (76 BCE–4 CE) served under Julius Caesar and then
under Antony. In 40 BCE, he helped bring the erstwhile partners in the Second
Triumvirate, Antony and Octavian, together again in the Treaty of Brundisium and,
though refusing to take up arms against Antony, later became a supporter of Octa-
vian. In 39, he was honored with a triumph for his victory over the Parthini, a tribe
in Illyria (= Dalmatia). He wrote a history of the tumultuous period from 60 to 42
BCE, as well as tragedies and erotic poems, and was a respected orator.

Right now you jar the ears with threatening blaring
from the war horns, now the trumpets blast,
    now dazzling arms bring terror to the
        skittish horses and their riders.

Great generals now I seem to see befouled
with dust of battle not inglorious
    and all of the world is vanquished
        but the dogged heart of Cato.[3]

Though Juno and the gods that favored
Africa in weakness left that country
    unavenged, they've brought the victor's grandsons
        as death offerings to Jugúrtha.[4]

What field that's richer from our Latin blood
does not proclaim with tombs our wicked strife
    and that the sound of ruin in the
        West is heard among the Persians?

What swirling main, what streams are unaware
of mournful war, what sea's not colored by
    the slaughter of the sons of Daunus?[5]
        What shore is without our bleeding?

But lest you put aside your jokes, my saucy
Muse, and sing once more a Cean dirge,[6]
    with me in Venus' grotto look for
        measures from a lighter plectrum.

3. Marcus Porcius Cato (95–46 BCE), a determined defender of the republic, after defeat in Africa at the battle of Thapsus, committed suicide rather than accept a pardon from Julius Caesar.

4. Jugurtha, king of Numidia, was defeated through the efforts of Gaius Marius and Lucius Cornelius Sulla and executed in Rome in 104 BCE.

5. Men from northern Apulia in southern Italy, where Horace was born (see Ode I.22).

6. A reference to Simonides of Ceos, a leading poet in the late sixth and early fifth centuries BCE and renowned for his ability to evoke pathos, as, for example, in his famous epigram for the Spartans who died at Thermopylae, fighting the Persians; "Stranger, tell the men of Lacedemon / we lie here obedient to their words."

II.2

Silver has no luster hidden in the
grudging earth, Sallústius Crispus,[1] you who
have not love of bullion, save for sober
  purpose it glistens.

Proculeíus[2] will live on to future
days, known for paternal care he'd shown his
brothers; lasting Fame will carry him on
  wings that do not fail.

Wider you can rule by conquering a
greedy heart than if you couple Libya to
far Cadiz and make both Africa and
  Spain serve one master.

Baleful dropsy grows in self-indulgence
nor can you slake parching thirst, unless the
cause of illness leaves the veins and wat'ry
  sickness the body.

Though once more Praháles[3] takes the throne of
Cyrus,[4] Virtue disagreeing with the

*Sapphic stanza*
1. Gaius Sallustius Crispus (d. 20 CE) was the great-nephew and adopted son of
the historian Sallust. He succeeded Maecenas as confidential advisor of Augustus.
2. Gaius Proculeius, another close advisor of Augustus, was famed for gener-
ously dividing his riches with his two brothers, who had lost their own wealth dur-
ing the civil wars.
3. Prahates (= Phraates IV), ruler of Parthia (ca. 38–3/2 BCE), who had to con-
tend with two revolts by the pretender Tiridates (see Ode I.26).
4. Cyrus the Great (d. 530) established the Achaemenid dynasty as the rulers of
central Asia and Asia Minor and, as a ruler, was regarded by the ancients with great
respect, as reflected in Xenophon's treatise on leadership, the *Cyropaedia* (*The Edu-
cation of Cyrus*).

crowd excludes him from the truly blessed[5] and
    teaches the people

not to use false words, bestowing kingdoms,
crowns, and laurel wreaths securely only
on whoever can behold great treasure
    and not glance backwards.

5. Stoicism teaches that only wisdom can make one a king and truly blessed.

II.3

Remember, keep a level head when on
the steep and likewise, when affairs go well,
    preserve a limit to excessive
        joy. For death is certain, Dellius,[1]

whether dejected you'll live all your days
or if at festivals on some secluded
    lawn reclining, you'll enjoy
        Falérnian that's aged and mellow.

To what end do the poplar and the lofty
pine delight to pair their gracious shade?
    Why does the rushing water strive to
        race within its winding channel?

Here order wine be brought and perfumed oils
and lovely blooms of roses all too brief,
    while time and circumstances and three
        sisters'[2] sable thread permit it.

You'll yield the woodlands you've bought up, your town-
house, and the villa by the yellow Tiber,
    you will yield, and then an heir will
        own the wealth that you have piled high.

It makes no difference whether born of ancient
stock or poor man of the lowest class,

*Alcaic stanza*
    1. Quintus Dellius was an active player during the civil wars and was so suc-
cessful moving from one side to the other, while maintaining his balance, that he
earned the nickname *desultor bellorum civilium* (leaping trick rider of the civil wars).
    2. The three goddesses (Parcae) who spin the thread of human fate.

you live your days to be a victim
   of a death that knows no pity.

We all are gathered to the selfsame place,
for soon or late the lot of each of us
   is shaken from the urn, and we must
      cross to everlasting exile.[3]

3. Ferried across the River Styx by Charon, boatman of the dead.

II.4

Do not be ashamed to love a servant,
Phocian Xánthias:[1] remember slave
Briséïs[2] with her fair complexion moved the
    haughty Achilles,

and the beauty of Tecméssa,[3] though a
captive, moved her master Ajax and mid
triumph Agamemnon lusted for a
    maiden he'd taken,[4]

after Troy's contingents fell before
Achilles' might and Hector's death gave weary
Greeks the citadel of Ílion more
    easily conquered.

You can't know: blond Phyllis[5] may have noble
parents, who will bring you honor;
certainly she mourns lost royalty and
    gods now turned hostile.

Rest assured the girl that you esteem is
not of base-born stock, and one so loyal,
so opposed to gain could never have a
    scandalous mother.

Lovely arms, a handsome face, and shapely
calves I praise unscathed: no need to be
suspicious of a man whose age has rushed to
    fill up four decades.

---

*Sapphic stanza*
    1. Phocis was a small city-state in central Greece, in which the shrine of Apollo at
Delphi was located. *Xanthias* is a masculine name for someone with fair hair.
    2. The captive woman given as a "prize" to Achilles but taken away by Agamem-
non in Book I of the *Iliad*.
    3. The daughter of King Teuthras of Mysia, near Troy.
    4. Cassandra, daughter of Priam, king of Troy.
    5. The name *Phyllis* is suggestive of dark green leaves (Greek *phulla*).

II.5

Not yet with neck subdued can she abide
the yoke, not yet can she match burdens with
    a ploughmate nor endure a bull
        upon her wild in love's rampage.

Your heifer's pleasure is amid the grassy
fields, now assuaging sultry heat
    in flowing streams, now desirous
        to frisk with calves in stands of

moist willow. Leave your longing for unmellowed
grapes: soon autumn in its varied colors
    will adorn for you the gray-blue
        clusters with a purple ripeness.

Soon she will follow you: for headstrong time
runs on and will give her the years it takes
    from you; soon Lálagë[1] with bold
        effrontery will seek a husband,

adored more than the flighty Phóloë,[2]
more than white-shouldered Chloris[3] shining like
    the polished moon that glitters on the
        sea at night, or Cnidian Gyges,[4]

whom if you set him in a group of girls,[5]
with flowing hair, with face androgynous,
    the blurring of distinctions would most
        wondrously deceive shrewd strangers.

*Alcaic stanza*
1. The name means "prattler."
2. Name used often of unwilling young women (see Ode I.33).
3. The name is from the Greek word for "greenish" or "pale green," and N-H (89)
note it "here suggests pallor" in reference to Chloris's white shoulders.
4. *Gyges*, a Lydian name, suggests voluptuousness and is reinforced by the refer-
ence to Cnidus on the coast of Ionia, associated with Aphrodite.
5. Like Achilles, hiding among the young women of Scyros (see Ode I.8).

## II.6

Septímius,[1] about to go with me to
far Cadiz and turbulent Cantábria[2]
and savage Syrtes' shoals,[3] where Moorish
    waters churn ever,

O that Tibur, founded by an Argive
colonist,[4] would be the home of my old
age, would be the end of weary roads and
    sea and campaigning.

If the Fates, unkind, prevent this, I will
seek the stream Galaésus[5] flowing sweet to
wooly flocks and countryside once ruled by
    Sparta's Phalánthus.[6]

That part of the world beyond the rest
delights me, where the honey does not yield to
Mount Hyméttus[7] and the olives challenge
    verdant Venáfrum,[8]

where Jove furnishes long springs and mild
winters and the valley Aulon[9] favoring

---

*Sapphic stanza*

1. The commentator Porphyrio indicates that Septimius was a Roman knight, and Suetonius's *Life of Horace* (30 ff. Rostagni) that he was a member of Augustus's inner circle.
2. Home to a warlike people living on the coast and mountains of northwest Spain.
3. Dangerous shoals along the coast of North Africa between Carthage and Cyrene, which today are in Tunisia and Libya, respectively.
4. Tiburnus.
5. Near Tarentum in south Italy.
6. Tarentum was founded by Phalanthus in 706 BCE.
7. Famed for its honey, Hymettus is just southeast of Athens.
8. City northeast of Naples in the valley of the Volturno.
9. Near Tarentum; the word *aulon* means "defile" or "glen" in Greek.

productive Bacchus envies least
Falérnian vineyards.[10]

That locale and blesséd refuge summon
you with me: there you will sprinkle with
accustomed tears the still warm ashes of the
bard who was your friend.

10. Falernian wine was a famous vintage from the Campania agricultural area
north of Naples.

II.7

O you who often with me had to face
the greatest risk when Brutus led our troops,
    who's brought you back a citizen to
        household gods and Italy's skies,

Pompeíus,[1] best of my companions, with whom
I often would break up the lingering day
    with wine, a garland in my hair made
        sleek with Syrian malobáthrum?[2]

With you I knew defeat and speedy flight
at Phílippi, my little shield abandoned,
    when our courage was undone and
        those once menacing were humbled:[3]

but midst the enemy swift Mercury
removed me fearful in a mantling mist;
    waves swallowed you again in war and
        carried you to seething waters.

Now pay to Jove the sacral feast you've pledged
and rest limbs wearied after long campaigning
    'neath my laurel tree nor spare the
        jars of wine I've readied for you.

Fill up smooth chalices with Massic vintage[4]
that allows you to forget. Pour out perfumes

*Alcaic stanza*
1. Who this Pompeius is is not clear, but like Horace he fought on the losing side
in the civil wars.
2. According to N-H (112), "an exotic spice, used as an unguent, deodorant, fla-
vouring, medicine, or soporific," originally from India.
3. Philippi is a city in northeastern Greece, where, in the fall of 42 BCE, Antony
and Octavian decisively defeated the forces of Brutus and Cassius, leading both to
commit suicide. The theme of throwing away one's shield to facilitate flight from
battle goes back to the early Greek poet Archilochus.
4. A fine wine from fertile Mount Massicus in the Campania in west central Italy
north of Naples.

from ample bottles. Who will hurry
  to make garlands from moist celery

or myrtle? Whom will Venus name as master
of the wine?[5] I'll play the Bacchant with
  Edónian frenzy.[6] With my friend
    returned, sweet is acting crazy.

5. The "master of the wine" (*arbiter* or *magister bibendi*), who oversaw the toasts
and the potency of the wine-to-water mixture, was selected by a throw of the dice
known as the "Venus throw" (*iactus Venerius*).
  6. The Edonians were a Thracian tribe noted for their wild, ecstatic worship of
Dionysus (= Bacchus) and hard drinking.

II.8

If you ever for your forsworn swearing
suffered any punishment, Barínë,[1]
if you were disfigured by a blemished
    nail or tooth turned black,

I would trust you: but as soon as you have
taken vows upon your perjured life, you
grow more fair and walk about, a public
    crisis for young men.

Helpful is the lie that's pledged upon your
mother's buried ashes and on all the
silent stars and sky at night and on the
    gods who are deathless.

Venus herself, I say, laughs at this, the
guileless Nymphs and cruel Cupid who is
always sharpening burning arrows on his
    blood-spattered whetstone.

All our youth are growing up for you, to
be in thrall to you, and former lovers
won't renounce their faithless mistress, often
    as they may threaten.

Mothers, thrifty graybeard fathers fear you,
fear you for their sons, and wretched maidens,
newly married, worry your allure will
    hinder their husbands.

*Sapphic stanza*
 1. The name means "girl from Bari," about which N-H comment (125): "The
word would retain its associations with the free-and-easy South, and the Greek ter-
mination suits a freedwoman."

## II.9

Not always do the rains pour down upon
bedraggled fields or fitful storms harass
    unceasingly the Caspian sea.
        In Armenia's territory,

friend Valgius,[1] lifeless ice does not
persist all year nor struggles of the oak-
    groves on Gargánus[2] with the North Winds
        nor the ash trees' loss of foliage:

you always in lamenting verses dwell
upon the loss of Mystes;[3] with the rising
    evening star and with its setting
        your devotion does not lessen.

Yet long-lived Nestor did not mourn for all
his days his dearly loved Antílochus[4]
    nor did his parents and his Phrygian
        sisters weep for youthful Troilus[5]

forever. Leave at last your delicate
complaints and let us celebrate instead
    new victories of Augustus Caesar
        near to rugged Mount Niphátes[6]

and how the river of the Persians,[7] added
to the conquered, flows with humbled waves
    and that the Scythian Gelóni
        are compelled to limit raiding.

*Alcaic stanza*
1. Gaius Valgius Rufus was a poet and close friend of Horace.
2. A mountain on a thumb of land that projects into the Adriatic in Apulia in southern Italy.
3. A masculine name meaning "initiate."
4. The young Greek warrior was slain while protecting his father, Nestor, from Memnon, an ally of the Trojans.
5. A younger son of Priam and Hecuba, king and queen of Troy, slain by Achilles.
6. In central Armenia.
7. The Euphrates.

II.10

More on course you'll keep your life, Licínius,[1]
not by always pushing out to sea nor,
while you dread the gales, by pressing hard the
    treacherous coastline.

One who cherishes the golden mean,
secure escapes the squalor of a shabby
hovel, soberly avoids the envy
    mansions elicit.

Giant pines more frequently are shaken
by the winds and soaring towers topple
down with greater loss and lightning strikes the
    summits of mountains.

Well prepared the heart that hopes in its
adversity, that fears in its success
another fate: for Jupiter again brings
    desolate winters

and removes them; if it now is grim, it
one day will not be: Apollo sometimes
with his lyre stirs the Muse and does not
    always draw his bow.[2]

Show yourself, when you're beset with trouble,
brave and full of spirit; wisely you will
trim your swollen sails, when winds may blow too
    much in your favor.

*Sapphic stanza*
    1. Usually identified with the outspoken Licinius Murena, brother-in-law of
Maecenas and consul in 23 BCE, who was removed from office and then implicated
in a conspiracy against Augustus. He was put to death after trying to escape.
    2. Apollo with his lyre is patron of music and poetry and with his bow, dealer of
destruction and plague.

## II.11

What warlike Spaniards and the Scythians
beyond the Adriatic are devising,
    Quínctius Hirpínus,[1] give up
        asking; don't be agitated

about a span of life that asks for little.
Smooth-faced youth and beauty swiftly pass,
    as withered age with graying temples
        thwarts love's play and easy slumber.

The bloom on flowers in the spring does not
remain forever nor the moon blush red
    with but one face. Why worry over
        plans that cannot be eternal?

Why not recline beneath a lofty plane
tree or this pine right now, and while we can,
    our gray hair scented with a rose,
        anointed with Assyrian nard oil,[2]

enjoy the wine? Let Bacchus scatter gnawing
cares. What servant boy will swiftly quench
    the cups of fiery Falérnian
        with freshly flowing water?[3]

Who will lure from her rooms the harlot Lydë?[4]
Go now, tell her hurry with her ivory
    lyre and her hair bound plainly
        in a bun in Spartan manner.

*Alcaic stanza*
    1. Quinctius is usually identified with the Quinctius addressed in Horace's
Epistles I.16. Hirpinus has often been interpreted as his cognomen, the final part
of his name, but N-H (167–68) see it as a geographic reference, meaning "Hir-
pinian." The Hirpini were an Italic people of south central Italy who bordered the
Samnites.
    2. Syria was well known for its perfumes.
    3. Like the Greeks, the Romans mixed their wine with water (cf. Ode II.7).
    4. Like the name *Lydia, Lyde* has voluptuous associations with the Lydian people
of Asia Minor (see also Odes III.11 and 28).

II.12

You would not want the grim Numántian war
nor iron Hannibal nor Sicily's
sea red with Punic blood adapted to
    the lyre's gentle strains[1]

nor savage Lapiths and Hylaéus, sottish
Centaur,[2] and the Giants mastered by
the hand of Hercules, when Saturn's shining
    palace trembled at

the danger.[3] It's better you should tell
in prose accounts of battles Caesar fought,
Maecénas, and of kings once menacing
    led through the streets in chains.

The Muse has wished I tell of sweet-voiced songs
of our Licýmnia,[4] her shining eyes,
and of her heart completely faithful in
    love's mutuality.

Not unbecomingly she lifts her foot
to dance and spars in jest and playfully
links arms with dazzling girls who gather on
    Diana's holy day.[5]

*Second Asclepiad system*
    1. The references are to three victorious Roman wars: the Celtiberian War in
Spain, culminating in the conquest of the fortress city Numantia in 133 BCE; the
Second Punic War (218–202 BCE), in which Hannibal was the most formidable
Carthaginian leader; and the First Punic War (264–241 BCE), in which naval battles
were prominent.
    2. At the wedding of Hippodamia with Pirithous, king of the Lapiths, the Cen-
taurs, who were among the invited guests, attempted to carry off the women,
including the bride.
    3. The Giants attempted to capture Olympus (= "Saturn's shining palace"), home
of the gods.
    4. Some scholars have seen in this name a hidden allusion to the wife of Mae-
cenas, Terentia, whose name has the same metrical value. As to the origin of the
name, a possible etymological connection has been suggested with the Greek word
for "sweet," *glukus* (the g before l tending not to be pronounced by Romans), and
*hymnein* (to sing) = "sweet singer" (see N-H, 194).
    5. Diana's festival was celebrated on August 13.

Now would you wish to trade the tresses of
Licýmnia for wealth of Persian kings
or the prosperity of Phrygia
    or Arab opulence,

when she inclines her neck to burning kisses
or with pliant cruelty denies
what she'd like stolen rather than requested
    and at times steals first?

II.13

He planted on an inauspicious day,
who with a hand accursed first raised you, tree,
    to visit death on his descendants
        and a scandal on the district.

I could believe he broke his father's neck
and in the middle of the night had splashed
    a guest's blood on the shrine that holds his
        household gods; he dealt in poisons

from Colchis[1] and whatever evil is
conceivable, the one who put you on
    my land, you dismal log, to fall
        upon your blameless master.

A man is never fully ready hour
by hour for what he would avoid. Phoenician
    sailors dread the Bosphorus but
        do not fear blind fate from elsewhere;

the soldier fears the arrows of the
Parthian attacking in retreat; Italian
    dungeons chill the Parthian, but
        unexpected death will take all.

I almost saw Prosérpina's dark kingdom
and lord Aéacus[2] dispensing judgment
    and the seats assigned the blest and
        with Aeólic lyre Sappho

complaining of the girls of Lesbos,[3] and,
more richly with your golden plectrum, you

---

*Alcaic stanza*
1. Home of the sorceress Medea, well known from the play of Euripides.
2. Proserpina was queen of the Underworld and Aeacus one of the three judges
of the dead.
3. Preserved poems of Sappho evidence such reproaches.

Alcaéus, singing of your ship storm-
tossed and ills of war and exile.[4]

The shades in reverent silence are in wonder
at the words of both, but, moving close
   the crowd prefers to drink in tales of
      battle and of tyrants banished.[5]

Why wonder, when bedazzled by those songs,
one-hundred-headed Cérberus[6] relaxes
   his black ears and serpents twined in
      hair of Furies find refreshment?

Yes, even Pelops's father and Prométheus
to the lovely sound distract their suffering
   and Oríon does not care to
      harry lions or shy lynxes.[7]

4. Alcaeus led a tumultuous life embroiled in the ups and downs of politics in his native city of Mitylene on the island of Lesbos (see also Ode I.14).

5. At least two banished tyrant rulers of Mitylene have a connection to Alcaeus: Melanchrus and Myrsilus.

6. The guardian dog of Hell is usually represented in the visual arts as having two or three heads, but in literature, of course, there were no limits to how he could be represented.

7. For transgressions against the gods, Tantulus, father of Pelops, the Titan Prometheus, and the great hunter Oríon were all condemned to punishment.

## II.14

Alas the fleeting years slip by, O
Póstumus,[1] nor will your piety delay
    the signs of old age pressing on and
        death that cannot be defeated,

not if each day that passes, friend, you would
appease unfeeling Pluto with three hundred
    oxen slain. He binds three-bodied
        Géryon[2] and Títyos[3] with

the gloomy waters of the underworld
we all must travel that enjoy the bounty
    of the earth, whether princes
        or impoverished tenant farmers.

In vain we'll keep from bloody warfare and
the howling Adriatic's crashing waves,
    in vain we'll fear the South Wind blowing
        pestilential in the Autumn.

You must behold Cocýtus'[4] black meanderings
on its sluggish course, the ill-famed daughters
    sired of Dánaüs and Sísyphus[5]
        condemned to endless labor;

you must forsake this earth, your home and cherished
wife, nor of these trees you cultivate

---

*Alcaic stanza*
1. This individual is unidentified, though N-H (223–24) offer as a possibility the Postumus who appears in *Propertius* III.12.
2. A monster whom Hercules slew in order to take his cattle during his Twelve Labors.
3. A Giant slain for assaulting Latona, mother of Apollo and Diana (= Artemis), and consigned to punishment in the Underworld.
4. River in the Underworld.
5. Forty-nine of the fifty daughters of Danaus were condemned eternally to fill a leaky jar in the Underworld for slaying their husbands on the orders of their father (see Ode III.11), and Sisyphus for his offenses against the gods was punished by having to roll a heavy rock uphill, only to have it roll down again when almost at the summit.

will any follow you, their fleeting
  master, but the hated cypress.[6]

An heir more worthy will consume your
Caécuban now guarded by a hundred keys
  and splash fine floors with haughty vintage
    better than at priestly banquets.

6. Cypress branches were placed at the door of a house of mourning and by the
altar and pyre at the funeral.

## II.15

Soon princely villas will allow few acres
for the plow, ponds everywhere will be
  observed extending wider than the
    Lucrine Lake,[1] while a bachelor plane tree

will oust the useful elms.[2] Then violets
and myrtle and all kinds of scents will sprinkle
  fragrance where once olive groves were
    fruitful for a former owner;

then laurel with abundant branches will
shut out the fiery rays. Not thus was it
  ordained by Romulus and rustic
    Cato[3] and our fathers' standards.

By choice their wealth was limited, the state's
possessions great; no private porticos
  of mammoth size were sited to
    receive the shade the north side offers,

nor would the laws allow them to despise
homes built of turf, while ordering by public
  means the walls[4] and temples be
    adorned with newly chiseled stone work.

---

*Alcaic stanza*

1. Just north of Naples.

2. In Roman viticulture vines were trained to grow on elms, while the spreading plane tree was cultivated for its shade by the wealthy. N-H point out (245) that "in the moral climate of Augustan Rome *caelebs* [= bachelor] has associations of uselessness and self-indulgence."

3. Marcus Porcius Cato (234–149 BCE), leading politician and literary figure of his day, was devoted to old-fashioned Roman values.

4. Interpreting with N-H (251) *oppida* as referring to city walls as "the most conspicuous monumental constructions of primitive Italy."

II.16

Peace he begs the gods for, caught upon the
wide Aegean, once black clouds have covered
up the moon and stars do not provide sure
        guidance for sailors,

peace the Thracian, furious in war, craves,
peace the Mede adorned with handsome quiver,[1]
peace, friend Grosphus,[2] which cannot be bought with
        gems, gold, or purple.

For not riches nor the consul's powers
can eliminate the heart's tormenting
turbulence and cares that flit around a
        fine paneled ceiling.

One lives well with little on whose slender
table glistens his ancestral salt
cellar, for whom not fear nor base desire
        disturbs his soft slumber.

Why with short lives do we boldly aim[3] so
high? Why pass to regions warmed by other
suns? What exile from his native land has
        also fled himself?

Baneful Care climbs onto bronze-clad galleys
nor abandons squads of cavalrymen,
Care that's swifter than deer or the East Wind
        driving cloud billows.[4]

Happy in the present, let your heart
disdain to care for what's to come and temper

---

*Sapphic stanza*
1. An Iranian people.
2. Pompeius Grosphus, a wealthy Sicilian landowner.
3. The name *Grosphus* in Greek means throwing spear, and at this point Horace
puns on the name with verb *iaculamur*, which means literally "we throw a javelin."
4. This stanza is bracketed as intrusive by K, but not by SB and N-H.

bitter times with easy laughter: nothing
    is blessed completely.

Early death dispatched far-famed Achilles,
his protracted age reduced Tithónus,[5]
and it's possible that time will bring me
    what it's denied you.

Yours in Sicily one hundred herds of
lowing cattle;[6] yours a mare that's ready
for a chariot; you dress in woolens
    twice dyed in murex

brought from Africa. Fate that does not
lie has given me my humble farm, my
slender Muse inspired in Greece, and scorn for
    the spiteful rabble.[7]

5. Tithonus was loved by Eos (Dawn), who gave him immortality but forgot to give him eternal youth, so he slowly shriveled away.

6. An alternate translation is: "Yours in Sicily one hundred flocks and / lowing cattle."

7. Because he was the son of a freedman, Horace experienced the ill will and envy of those less accomplished.

II.17

Why are you killing me with your complaints?
It does not suit the gods nor me that you
    die first, Maecénas, you who honor
        me with your support and friendship.

Ah, if you are carried off before
me—half my soul—why should I linger, not
    so dear to any and no longer
        whole? That day will bring the ruin

of both of us. I have not sworn a lying
oath: for we will go, yes, we will go,
    whenever you will lead, comrades
        ready for the final journey.

Not the Chimaéra's[1] fiery breath, not
one hundred-handed Gyges'[2] reappearance
    will divert me ever: so the
        Fates decree and mighty Justice.

Whether Libra or dread Scorpio
embody the more fearful portion of
    my horoscope or Capricorn the
        ruler of the western waters,

our stars in some amazing way are in
alignment: for resplendent Jupiter's
    protection wrested you from wicked
        Saturn and delayed the swift wings

of Fate, when in the theater people thronging
raised aloud a joyful sound three times:[3]

*Alcaic stanza*
    1. Composite monster, "lion in front, snake behind, she-goat in the middle" (*Iliad*
VI.181), killed by Bellerophon.
    2. A Giant punished in the Underworld.
    3. At the time Maecenas recovered from illness (see Ode I.20).

>  while I was brained to death, the victim
>      of a falling tree, had Faunus[4]

> not eased the blow, the guardian of those
> who follow Mercury.[5] Remember to
>      repay with votive shrine and offerings:
>          I will slay a modest ewe lamb.

4. Faunus (= Pan), a Roman god of the forests and protector of flocks; for the deadly tree, see Ode II.13.

5. As the god of eloquence Mercury is the patron of poets (see Ode I.10). Faunus was the son of Mercury.

II.18

Neither ivory nor golden
    coffered ceilings glitter in my
house, nor do Hyméttan beams[1]
    press down on columns cut in farthest

Africa nor am I unknown
    heir to Attalus's palace,[2]
nor do well-born ladies trail
    for me their cloth of finest purple.

Yet I've honor and a generous
    vein of talent, and the rich man
seeks me out though poor. I press
    the gods for nothing else nor beg an

influential friend for more:
    I'm blessed enough with Sabine country.
One day treads upon another,
    and new moons persist in waning:

you contract for marble to
    be cut, though death's close by, and heedless
of the grave you pile up houses,
    and you strain to push the clamoring

sea from Baiae's coast,[3] not feeling
    wealthy while the shore confines you.
What about it that you keep
    on plucking up your neighbor's boundary

stones and in your greed encroach
    upon your clients' holdings? Wife and

---

*Hipponactean system (trochaic meter)*
1. Gray-blue marble from Mount Hymettus, near Athens.
2. At his death in 133 King Attalus III of Pergamum bequeathed to Rome his kingdom, which became the province of Asia.
3. Roman resort town near Naples.

husband, bearing household gods
and ragged children, are cast out.

Still no palace waits upon
the wealthy man more certainly than
that of ravening Death. Why
contend for further property? An

equal piece of land lies open
to the poor man and the sons of
kings, nor did Death's servant, bribed
by gold, bring back[4] Prométheus. He

holds confined proud Tántalus
and Tántalus's offspring;[5] called and
not called to relieve the poor
man done with laboring, he listens.

4. Keeping *revexit* (did bring back) with SB, K, and most of the manuscripts and
interpreting *satelles Orci* (Death's servant) as the ferryman of the dead, Charon,
while N-H (310–12) accept the reading *revinxit* (did unbind) and interpret *satelles
Orci* as Mercury, which would translate "nor . . . did Death's servant [= Mercury]
unbind."
5. For trangressions against the gods, Tantalus, father of Pelops and ancestor of
the cursed House of Atreus, was condemned to eternal hunger and thirst in the
presence of food and drink.

## II.19

Among secluded cliffs, believe me, future
generations, I saw Bacchus teaching
    songs to listening nymphs and to sharp
        ears of cloven-footed satyrs.

Euhoe, my mind is trembling with new fear
and eddying in joy, my heart filled up
    with Bacchus; euhoe, spare me Liber,[1]
        feared for your stern thyrsus,[2] spare me.

It is permitted that I sing of your
relentless votaries and springs of wine
    and lavish streams of milk and
        honey poured from hollow tree trunks,

permitted that I sing of Ariádne's
crown[3] you've added to the stars and Pentheus'
    palace dashed to ruin and the
        doom of Thracian king Lycúrgus.[4]

You bend back rivers, turn barbarian seas;
intoxicated on Parnassus with
    a knot of serpents without injury
        you bind the hair of Maenads.

And you, when the wicked company
of Giants scaled your father's kingdom on
    Olympus, you hurled Rhoetus back with
        lion's claws and fearsome muzzle,

*Alcaic stanza*

1. Italian fertility god identified with Greek god Dionysus/Bacchus.

2. A wand with ivy and vine leaves twined round with a pinecone at the top, borne by Dionysus and his followers.

3. After Ariadne was abandoned by the Athenian hero Theseus on the island of Naxos, Dionysus rescued her, married her, and made her immortal, her bridal crown being set among the stars.

4. Both Kings Pentheus of Thebes and Lycurgus of Thrace were punished for their refusal to respect the divinity of Dionysus.

although, as if more suited to the dance
and jokes and play, you were alleged to be
    less fitted for a fight; but you to
        peace and war alike were party.

A harmless Cérberus[5] beheld you fair
with horn[6] of gold; he gently rubbed his tail
    against you, licked your feet and shins with
        triple tongues as you departed.

5. The guardian dog of Hell, usually represented in the visual arts as having two
or three heads, but in Ode II.13 with one hundred heads. Bacchus went down to
Hades to rescue his mother Semele.
   6. A horn was an attribute of animal power.

II.20

On wings not weak or common, I a bard
of double nature[1] will be carried through
    clear air nor will I linger longer
        on the earth. Surpassing envy,

I'll leave behind the cities. I, the child
of humble folk, I whom you summon, dear
    Maecénas, I will not meet death nor
        be hemmed in by Stygian waters.

Already now the skin is roughening on
my shins and I'm transformed into a swan
    as on my fingers and my shoulders
        there begin to sprout light feathers.

Now better known than Ícarus the son
of Daédalus,[2] songbird, I'll travel to
    the groaning Bosphorus and Afric
        Syrtes[3] and the northern tundra:

the Colchian, the Dacian who pretends
no fear of Roman forces, and the far

---

*Alcaic stanza*

1. Being both man and bird.

2. The skilled craftsman was famed for creating wings for himself and his son, Icarus, so that they could escape imprisonment on Crete. Icarus flew too near the sun, and the wax binding his wings melted, causing him to fall to his death in the eastern Aegean Sea, which took his name.

3. Dangerous shoals along the coast of North Africa between Carthage and Cyrene, which today are in Tunisia and Libya, respectively.

Gelóni[4] will come to know me, the
    Gaul will learn and skillful[5] Spaniard.

Away with dirges at my empty
    burial, unseemly mourning, and complaints;
        restrain the wailing and omit
            unnecessary funeral offerings.

4. The Colchians, Dacians, and Geloni were foreign peoples beyond Rome's
jurisdiction at this time.
   5. Interpreting *peritus* (skillful) as a reference to a level of Roman culture in
Spain that within the next hundred years would produce a distinguished series of
Latin writers.

# BOOK III

III.1

I hate the uninitiated mob
and fend it off. Now keep silent: as
    the Muses' priest, songs before
        unheard I sing to lads and maidens.

The power of dread kings is on their flocks,
on kings themselves there is the power of Jove,
    who, glorious from his conquest of the
        Giants,[1] moves all with an eyebrow.

It's true that one man may arrange his vines
more widely spaced; another with more noble
    lineage strive for office; this one
        through his greater fame and virtue

contend; another have a larger
entourage: with equal law Necessity
    selects by lot the great and lowly;
        her urn holds the name of each one.

For whom the unsheathed saber dangles by
his wicked neck,[2] Sicilian feasts will not
    contrive a taste that's sweet, the melody
        of birds' songs and the lyre

*Alcaic stanza*
This poem and the five succeeding, all in Alcaic stanzas, because of their themes,
are commonly known as the Roman Odes.
    1. The Giants, the huge sons of Earth, attempted to overthrow the Olympian gods
but were defeated with the help of Hercules.
    2. Reference to the story of Damocles, a courtier of the Sicilian ruler Dionysius
II (fourth century BCE), who admired the apparent good fortune of his master but
was made to recognize the risks when a sword, hanging by a thread, was dangled
over his head as he enjoyed a royal feast.

will not restore his sleep; the gentle sleep
of country folk does not disdain their humble
    dwellings and a shady bank or
        valleys ruffled by the Zephyrs.

For one who longs for what's sufficient, neither
raging sea nor savage onset of
    October weather, with the setting
        Bear or rising Kid, is troubling,[3]

nor is the vineyard buffeted by hail
nor the deceitful farm, on which the trees
    accuse now rains, now parching summer
        heat, now adverse winter weather.

The fish can feel the sea confined when massive
stones are heaped upon the deep; here
    the contractor with workers, and the
        owner, tired of his land, lay

down rubble fill; but Fear and Menace climb
in concert with the owner, nor does gloomy
    Care depart a bronze-sheathed galley;
        it sits behind the horseman.

But if not Phrygian marble[4] nor the use
of purple raiment brighter than the stars
    assuages grief nor fine Falérnian[5]
        nor royal Persian perfumes,

why build a lofty hall with columns to
be envied in a style that is new?
    Why should I trade my Sabine valley
        for more labored-over riches?

---

3. Because he will not be traveling the seas as a merchant.
4. A white marble with purple markings.
5. A wine from Campania of the highest quality.

III.2

Let the lad grown tough from harsh campaigning
learn to bear privation willingly
    and, as a horseman dreaded for his
        spear, harass fierce Parthians[1] and

live life exposed to danger under open
skies. Looking at him from the hostile
    fortress, let the warring ruler's
        wife and grownup daughter murmur,

"alas," lest, new to combat, her intended
prince incite the lion hard to handle
    whom a bloody fury hurtles
        through the middle of the carnage.

To die for native land is sweet and fitting:
death pursues the man who flees and does
    not spare the hamstrings[2] and the trembling
        back of youth avoiding battle.

Manliness, untouched by an election
loss, shines bright, its honors still intact,
    nor at the people's fickle whim takes
        on or puts aside an office.

Manliness, which opens heaven to
those worthy not to die, ventures travel
    by a path denied and spurns on
        wings the common herd and damp ground.

For faithful silence recompense is sure:
I shall forbid the one revealing Ceres'

---

*Alcaic stanza*
1. The Parthian dynasty, the Arsacids, ruled from the Euphrates to the Indus from 247 BCE to 224 CE, and their most effective forces were horse archers.
2. In ancient warfare, it was common to strike a fleeing enemy in the hamstrings.

sacred mysteries[3] to be
  beneath my roof or to set sail in

my fragile craft: for often, when neglected,
Jupiter has joined the pure to tainted;
  Justice, though lame, rarely lets go
    of the wicked who precede her.

---

3. The secret initiation rites in the worship of Demeter (= Ceres) and her daughter Kore (= Proserpina), most famously centered on Eleusis in the territory of Athens.

III.3

A man that's just and steadfast in resolve
no fevered citizenry with perverse
    demands, no threatening despot shakes from
        his firm purpose nor the South Wind,

rough ruler of the restless Adriatic
nor the mighty hand of fulminating
    Jove: if smashed the sky should topple,
        fearless he will face the ruin.

Thus Pollux and wide wand'ring Hercules
in struggle reached the fiery citadels,[1]
    with whom Augustus will recline and
        will with ruddy lips drink nectar;

thus through your merit, with a yoke on their
reluctant necks your tigers, father Bacchus,
    carried you, thus Romulus
        avoided Hades through Mars' horses,[2]

when Juno gave a speech that satisfied
the gods in council: "He the fateful, unchaste
    judge, and she the foreign woman,
        Ílion, turned Ílion to

"ashes,[3] condemned by me and chaste Minerva
with its people and deceitful ruler
    from the time Laómedon had
        duped the gods of promised payment.[4]

*Alcaic stanza*
1. The heights of heaven.
2. One tradition declared that Romulus was carried to heaven by the chariot of Mars.
   3. The reference is, of course, to the Judgment of Paris, where the Trojan prince Paris declared Venus the winner in a beauty contest with Juno and Minerva, after Venus had bribed Paris by offering him Helen, the most beautiful of women and wife of Menelaus, king of Sparta. By carrying Helen off to Troy (= Ilion), Paris incited the Trojan War, which led to the city's destruction.
   4. Laomedon, king of Troy, after arranging for Poseidon and Apollo (= Phoebus) to build his city's walls, refused to pay for the work.

"No longer her notorious host bedazzles
the adulteress from Sparta, no longer
   does Priam's lying house through Hector's
     aid repel Achaéan fighters:

"the war protracted by our strife has ceased:[5]
at once for Mars's sake I'll give up my painful
   anger and forgive my hated
     grandson,[6] whom the Trojan priestess

"has borne. That man I will permit to pass
unto the seats of light, to taste the juice
   of nectar, and to be enrolled
     among the gods' serene assembly.

"As long as ample sea may rage mid Rome
and Ílion, blessed let the exiles rule
   in any place they wish; as long as
     on the graves of Priam and Paris

"the cattle caper and the wild beasts
conceal their whelps unchallenged, may the shining
   Capitol[7] remain and warrior
     Rome command defeated Persians.

"Feared widely may she spread her name to farthest
coastlines, where a narrow strait keeps
   Africa apart from Europe, where the
     swollen Nile waters cropland.

"Gold undiscovered and thus better placed,
 while earth conceals it, she is stronger in
   rejecting than despoiling for
     human uses all things sacred.

5. The gods took sides during the Trojan War.
6. Romulus, son of Mars and the Vestal Virgin Ilia, descendant of Aeneas.
7. The Capitoline Hill, Rome's most holy spot, site of the major temple to Jupiter and important shrines, as well as the city's original citadel, the *arx*.

"Whatever limit circumscribes the world,
   she will reach with her weapons, eager to
      explore where fires are run riot,
         where mist and showers gather.

"But to the warlike Romans I declare
   their fate on this condition that they, puffed up
      in their piety and power, not
         chose to reconstruct ancestral

"Troy. Inauspiciously reborn, Troy's doom
   will be repeated with grim bloodletting
      as I, Jove's wife and sister, lead on
         the victorious battalions.

"If thrice its brazen wall should rise again
   through Phoebus' aid, thrice let it perish smashed
      by my Achaéans and thrice the captive
         wife[8] should mourn her sons and husband."

But no, this does not suit a playful lyre.
Where are you heading, Muse? Cease stubbornly
   to narrate speeches of the gods and
      lessen great themes with slight verses.

8. The image of the suffering of captive Trojan wives was familiar to both Greeks and Romans, especially from the plays of Euripides, like the *Trojan Women, Andromache,* and *Hecuba.* Queen Hecuba, in particular, wife of slaughtered King Priam and mother of many slain sons, comes readily to mind.

III.4

Descend from heaven, queen Callíopë,[1]
and phrase lengthy song upon the pipe,
   or now with ringing voice if you
      prefer, or on Apollo's lyre.

Do you hear her? Or does a lovely madness
trick me? I seem to hear her and to wander
   through a sacred grove amidst which
      pleasant streams and breeze are stirring.

The fabled ringdoves[2] on Apúlian Vultur,
past the doorstep of nurse Púllia,[3]
   covered me with fresh, green leaves, a
      child tired out from sleep and

from play: it was a marvel to whoever
occupy the aerie of high
   Acerúntia or the Bantine meadows
      or low-lying rich Foréntum,[4]

how I could sleep, my body safe from deadly
vipers and from bears, how I was swathed
   in sacred laurel mixed with myrtle,[5]
      not without the gods, a brave boy.

Yours, Muses, yours I climb among the lofty
Sabine hills, or if Praenéste's[6] chilly

---

*Alcaic stanza*

1. Muse whose name means "beautiful-voiced." N-R comment (57): The Greek
poet "Hesiod described Callíopë as the most important (*propherestatē*) of the Muses
(*theog.* 79)."

2. Another name for this bird is the wood-pigeon (*Columba palumbus*).

3. This is assumed to be the name of Horace's childhood nurse, but there is
much dispute about this line of the stanza.

4. Vultur, Aceruntia, Bantia, and Forentum were all places near to Venusia in the
heart of that part of southern Italy where Horace was born.

5. Laurel was sacred to Apollo and myrtle to Venus.

6. A city about twenty miles southeast of Rome on a spur of the Apennines, site
of the great Temple of Fortuna.

reaches please me or the slopes of
Tibur or unclouded Baiae.[7]

Through my devotion to your dances and
your springs, defeat at Phílippi[8] did not
   destroy me, nor the cursèd tree[9] nor
      Palinúrus' wat'ry headland.[10]

Whenever you are with me, willingly
a sailor I will try the raving
   Bosphorus or travel through the burning
      sands along the Syrian coastline.

I'll visit Britons cruel to strangers and
the Cóncani[11] who drink a horse's blood,
   visit Gelóni[12] bowmen and will
      reach the Scythian Don[13] in safety.

You, once he's settled his war-weary legions
in the towns, you refresh in your
   Piérian[14] cave great Caesar
      seeking to conclude his labors.

You, kindly goddesses, give gentle counsel
and take pleasure giving it. We know
   how he[15] with thunderbolts destroyed the
      wicked Titans and vast Giants,[16]

7. Coastal resort near Naples.
   8. Site of the final defeat of Brutus and Cassius by Antony and Octavian in 42
BCE (see Ode II.7).
   9. See Ode II.13.
   10. A promontory on the Tyrrhenian sea in Lucania in the south of Italy, where
ships of Octavian were destroyed in a storm during his war with Pompey's son,
Sextus, at a time when Maecenas may have been in attendance and accompanied
by Horace.
   11. A tribe of the Cantabri in the northwest of Spain.
   12. A Scythian tribe.
   13. "Regarded as the boundary of Europe and Asia" (N-R, 68).
   14. Pieria in Macedonia, north of Mount Olympus, was earliest identified as the
home of the Muses.
   15. Jupiter.
   16. The Titans were an earlier generation of gods overthrown in battle by the
Olympians led by Zeus (= Jupiter). The Giants, the huge sons of Earth, attempted

he who controls calm earth and windy seas,
he who alone with his just power rules
    the shades and the grim kingdom of the
        dead, and gods and throngs of mortals.

Immense alarm those youth[17] relying on
their teeming arms provoked in Jove as did
    the brothers[18] who attempted to pile
        Pélion upon Olympus.

But what could mighty Mimas and Typhoéus
do or towering Porphýrion,
    what Rhoetus or Encéladas,[19]
        boldly hurling torn-up tree trunks,

rushing against the thund'ring aegis of
Minerva?[20] Here stood eager Volcan, here
    too lady Juno and the god who
        never puts aside his bow,

who in the pure Castálian waters[21] bathes
his unbound hair, who dwells in Lycian thickets
    and his natal woodlands, Delian
        and Pátaran Apollo.[22]

Force lacking judgment falls by its own weight,
while force controlled the gods raise higher still,
    but they abominate the forces
        moving in the heart all evil.

---

to overthrow the Olympian gods but were defeated with the help of Hercules. The
Titans and the Giants were often confused.

    17. The Giants.

    18. The Giants Otus and Ephialtes, who tried to climb to heaven by piling the
Thessalian mountains Pelion and Ossa upon Olympus.

    19. All five are Giants.

    20. Minerva/Athena is usually represented with a helmet and with the aegis, a
goat skin with a Gorgon's head in the middle and fringed with snakes, worn over
the breast to provide protection and to inspire fear in enemies.

    21. The Castalian Spring, sacred to Apollo and the Muses, is at Apollo's shrine at
Delphi.

    22. Delos was the birth place of Apollo and his sister Diana (= Artemis), and Pat-
ara in Lycia on the south coast of Turkey was the site of one of his oracular shrines.

A hundred-handed Gyges[23] is a witness
to my thoughts, as is Oríon, famed
   assailant of unstained Diana,
      mastered by the maiden's arrow.

Earth piled upon her monster-offspring grieves
and mourns that with a thunderbolt they've been
   dispatched to ashen Orcus;[24] neither
      has swift fire gnawed through Aetna

imposed above[25] nor has the bird assigned
to guard his foulness left the liver of
   licentious Títyus;[26] Piríthöus[27]
      the lover countless chains bind.

23. A Giant punished in the Underworld who also appears in Ode II.17.
24. The Underworld.
25. Aetna was piled upon the Giants after their defeat.
26. A Giant slain for assaulting Latona (= Leto), mother of Apollo and Diana, and consigned to punishment in the Underworld by having his liver, regarded as the seat of desire, forever eaten by two vultures.
27. Pirithous, king of the Lapiths, with his friend Theseus of Athens, attempted to carry off Queen Proserpina (= Persephone) from the Underworld but was caught and imprisoned there.

## III.5

It's our belief that Jove rules thundering
in heaven: here on earth Augustus will
    be held a god with Britons and grim
        Persians added to the empire.

Have soldiers of defeated Crassus[1] lived
disgraced by marriage to barbarian wives
    —O Senate, O our values betrayed!—
        and grown old with foreign weapons

while serving Persia's king, a Marsian or
Apúlian[2] who's forgotten sacred shields,[3]
    his name and toga and eternal
        Vesta, though Rome and Jove are safe?

This Régulus[4] with foresight had provided
for, opposing infamous arrangements
    and a precedent that brought with
        it destruction to the future,

if captured youths were not allowed to die
unpitied: "I have seen our standards hung

---

*Alcaic stanza*

    1. Marcus Licinius Crassus, a member of the First Triumvirate with Pompey and Julius Caesar, hoping to strengthen his reputation as a soldier, attempted to invade Parthia but met total defeat and was killed at Carrhae in 53 BCE. His soldiers who survived were taken prisoner by the Parthians.

    2. The Marsians, a tribe of central Italy, and the Apulians of southern Italy were famed as hardy soldiers.

    3. The *ancilia*, shields carried by the Salian priests and sacred to the Roman state since the time of King Numa.

    4. Marcus Atilius Regulus led an ultimately unsuccessful invasion of Africa during the First Punic War and was captured by the Carthaginians with his army in 255 BCE. He was eventually paroled and with an oath to return was sent from Carthage to Rome to arrange a prisoner exchange. He recommended to the Roman Senate not to agree to the exchange and then went back to Carthage, where he died by torture.

in Carthaginian temples and the
armor taken from our soldiers

"without bloodshed. I've seen our citizens,
once free, with hands tied up behind their backs
and gates not shut and fields once ravaged
by our troops now cultivated.

"Redeemed with gold a soldier will, no doubt,
return more fierce: with shame you couple loss!
The wool that's dyed with purple stain will
not again show its lost color

"nor can true courage be restored, when once
it has been lost, for those that are diminished;
if a doe untangled from thick
nets fights back, he will be gallant,

"who has submitted to the faithless foe,
and he will drub the Carthaginians
in future war, who feckless felt his
arms in shackles and has feared death.

"Unmindful whence he was to win his life,
he's mingled war with peace: O disgrace!
O mighty Carthage magnified by
Italy's ignoble ruin!"

It's said he turned away his chaste wife's kiss
and little sons, as one who'd lost the right
to be a citizen, and grimly
fixed upon the ground his manly

gaze, till he firmed the wavering senators
with counsel never given otherwise
and midst the mourning of his friends he
hurried off a splendid exile.

And yet he was aware of what the Punic
torturer was planning: nonetheless

he pushed aside his kinsman and the
    people slowing his return,

as if he, with a case decided, left
behind the lengthy business of his clients,
    heading to Venáfrum's fields or
        to Lacónian Taréntum.[5]

---

5. Both Venafrum, northeast of Naples, and Tarentum, a Spartan foundation in
the instep of Italy, were attractive locales (see Ode II.6).

## III.6

You will pay, Roman, undeservedly
for failures of your ancestors, until
    you have restored the gods' collapsing
        shrines and statues fouled with black smoke.

Because you bow before the gods, you rule.
In them find each beginning and conclusion:
    gods, neglected, have bestowed on
        mournful Italy much evil.

Now twice Monaéses and the band of
Pácorus[1] have crushed our inauspicious onslaughts
    and are happy adding captured
        plunder to their meager trappings;

the Dacian and Egyptian almost wrecked
the city taken up with factiousness,[2]
    the latter dreaded for his fleet, the
        former better with swift arrows.

The generations, bountiful in sin,
first tainted marriage, family, and the home:
    deriving from this source, disaster
        flowed upon our land and people.

The grown-up girl delights to learn Ionic[3]
dances and already now is formed
    in artifice and meditates on
        impure passion to the utmost.

*Alcaic stanza*

1. Pacorus and Monaeses were Parthian military commanders involved in the defeats of Antony's forces in 40 and 36 BCE, respectively.

2. Dacians, warring tribes in the lower Danube, supported Antony before the battle of Actium in 31 BCE, where the forces of Antony and Cleopatra's Egyptians went down to final defeat.

3. The Ionians, the Greeks settled on the west coast of Asia Minor, were identified with voluptuousness and excess.

She soon seeks after younger paramours
amid her husband's wine nor chooses
     hurriedly with lamps removed to
          whom she'd give forbidden pleasures,

but, summoned openly, her husband quite
aware, she rises if a peddler asks
     or if a master of a Spanish
          ship, rich buyer of dishonor.

Not born of parents such as these the youth
that stained the sea with Punic blood[4] and cut
     down Pyrrhus and the great Antíochus
          and Hannibal the fearsome,[5]

but manly sons of farmer soldiers, taught
to hoe the soil with a Samnite[6] mattock
     and, at their mother's stern command, to
          cut and carry firewood as

the sun was changing shadows on the mountains
and removing yokes from weary oxen,
     bringing on that welcome hour
          when the evening was approaching.

What has time's baneful passage not reduced?
Our fathers' days worse than our grandfathers'
     have rendered us more worthless, soon to
          bring forth offspring still more vicious.

---

4. During the First Punic War (264–241 BCE).

5. Pyrrhus (319–272 BCE), king of Epirus, Antiochus III (ca. 242–187 BCE), ruler of the Seleucid Empire, and Hannibal (247–183/2 BCE), leading Carthaginian general during the Second Punic War, were among the foremost military opponents Rome faced during her rise to power in the third and second centuries BCE, and they met defeat (and in that sense were "cut down," though not themselves killed) at the hands of Rome.

6. The Samnites were the Oscan-speaking peoples of Central Italy, including the original inhabitants of Horace's hometown Venusia. Oscan is an Italic language related to Latin.

III.7

Why weep, Astérië,[1] for one the cloudless
Zephyr will restore in early spring
   enriched with Asian goods, a
      youth of faithful constancy,

your Gyges?[2] Driven by the South Wind to
Epírus[3] in tempestuous fall weather,
   he spends freezing nights,
      unsleeping and with many tears.

But his tense hostess's sly messenger,
declaring wretched Chloë[4] sighs and burns
   with fires like your own,
      tempts him in a thousand ways.

He narrates how the naive Proetus' faithless
wife with lying charges rushed her husband
   towards the murder of the
      over-chaste Bellérophon;

he tells of Peleus almost done to death,
when steadfastly he shunned Hippólyta;[5]
   and he deceitfully spins
      stories teaching him to sin,

in vain: more deaf than cliffs on Ícarus,[6]
he hears the words and is unmoved. But you

*Third Asclepiad system*
1. The name means "starry."
2. This Lydian name suggests voluptuousness.
3. Ancient travelers for safety tended to hug the coastline, in this case the west coast of Greece, before crossing the Adriatic to Italy.
4. The hostess Chloe's name means "the first green shoot of plants" in spring and suggests freshness and immaturity.
5. Both the heroes Bellerophon and Peleus were victims of their hosts' wives who fell in love with them, but, not having their love reciprocated, accused the men of rape and put them in danger of being killed by the angry husbands.
6. Rocky island in the middle of the Aegean.

    beware Enípeus[7] next door
       please you more than would be right,

although no other on the Field of Mars
is viewed as so adroit in horsemanship
    nor is there any who can
       swim so swiftly Tiber's stream.

As night comes on, lock up your house and at
the playing of the plaintive flute, don't look
    into the street and, though he
       often calls you "hard," hold firm.

---

7. According to Quinn (260), the name of a river in Thessaly, but perhaps intended to remind the reader of the Greek word *enipē* (rebuke, reproach), with the meaning " 'reproacher' (i.e., one who reproaches Asterie for her constancy to Gyges)."

## III.8

March the first—it's Wives' Feast[1]—and you wonder
what am I, a bachelor, doing, what the
flowers and the incense mean, and charcoal
    on the turf altar,

you, a man who's learned in both Greek and
Latin: I had vowed to Liber[2] a sweet
banquet and white goat, when almost done to
    death by the tree's blow.[3]

This celebratory day within the
year will lift the cork secured with pitch out
of the bottle mellowed in the smoke when
    Tullus was consul.[4]

Take a hundred cups, Maecénas, honoring
your friend unscathed; keep the lamps on
watch till light: banish far from here all
    shouting and anger.

Put aside your statesmanlike concerns
about the City: Dacian Cótiso's force
is destroyed;[5] the Persians are at odds and
    fighting each other;

*Sapphic stanza*
1. The Matronalia celebrated by married women in honor of Juno Licinia, goddess of childbirth.
2. As N-R note (126–27), "Elsewhere H attributes his escape to Faunus (2.17.28) or the Muses (3.4.27). Liber combines both associations: he was a rustic god and, like Bacchus, . . . he could be represented as a patron of poets" (*epist.* 1.19.3). The name *Liber* means "free," which N-R point out "suits the god who delivered H from danger."
3. See Ode II.13.
4. Smoke was thought to improve wine. Lucius Volcacius Tullus was consul in 66 BCE and his son of the same name consul in 33 BCE. N-R (128) think the latter more likely.
5. Dacia (modern Romania), however, did not become a part of the Roman Empire until the reign of Trajan more than a century later.

the Cantábrian, old foe along the
Spanish coast, subdued at last, is docile;
Scythians, their bows unstrung, intend to
    pull back from the plains.

Heedless if the people somewhere struggle,
privately do not be too on guard:
enjoy the gifts the present hour offers:
    leave what is weighty.

III.9

"As long as I appealed to you
     nor did some youth more favored put his arms
around your glistening white neck,
     I lived more blessedly than Persia's king."

"As long as you were not more scorched
     by someone else and Lydia was
not scorned for Chloë,[1] much renowned,
     I lived more famed than Roman Ília."[2]

"Now Thracian Chloë governs me,
     adept at lovely songs, skilled with the lyre,
for whom I will not fear to die,
     if fate will spare dear heart and let her live."

"Cálaïs,[3] son of Órnytus
     of Thúrii,[4] with shared flame parches me,
for whom I'll suffer twice to die
     if fate will spare the lad and let him live."

"What if my former love returns
     and forces us beneath the brazen yoke,
if flaxen[5] Chloë is dislodged
     and for spurned Lydia the door stands wide?"

"Although that fellow's fairer than
     a star and you are lighter than a cork,
more testy than the Adriatic,
     gladly I would live or die with you."

*Fourth Asclepiad system*
This poem is a dialogue between a man and a woman, alternating with each
stanza, beginning with the man.
     1. The name *Lydia* has voluptuous associations with the people of Asia Minor
(see also Odes I.8, 13, and 25). The name *Chloe* means "the first green shoot of
plants" in spring and suggests freshness and immaturity (see Ode I.23).
     2. The mother of Romulus and Remus (see Ode I.2).
     3. The name seems to derive from the Greek word *kalos* (handsome, beautiful).
     4. Greek city in southern Italy.
     5. N-R note (139): "It may . . . be relevant that Chloe is described as a Thracian
(9), for the Romans admired the fair hair of northern women."

III.10

If, married, Lycë,[1] to a brutish man,
you drank the waters of the distant Don,
you'd still deplore exposing me to northern
    storms by your cruel gates.

Do you not hear how noisily the door,
how noisily the grove around your lovely
house is groaning to the wind, and Jove
    is freezing fallen snow?

Put off that pride disliked by Venus, lest
the wheel run back and rope fly off:[2] No Tuscan[3]
father sired you adverse to suitors,
    like Penelope.[4]

Although no gifts, no prayers, no lovers' purple
tinted pallor nor your husband smitten
by a mistress from Piéria[5]
    can bend you, may you spare

your suppliants, though you're not softer than
hard oak nor kinder in your heart than Moorish
serpents: not always will this flank endure
    your threshold or the rain.

*Second Asclepiad system*
This poem is modeled on the *paraklausithyron,* the locked-out lover's lament at
his mistress's door.
    1. *Lyce* means "wolf" in Greek.
    2. Metaphor of a pulley coming undone.
    3. Tuscan (= Etruscan) has here the connotation (1) of being licentious or (2) of
being of noble birth—both interpretations have been proposed.
    4. The faithful wife of Odysseus, who, during the absence of her husband,
refused to yield to the importuning of her suitors who wanted to succeed to Odys-
seus's kingdom.
    5. A part of Macedon north of Olympus, connected with the Muses.

III.11

Mercury[1]—for, taught by you, Amphíon[2]
moved the stones of Thebes through song—and you, O
tortoise shell, that resonates to seven
    strings so adeptly—

you once silent and unpleasing, now
beloved in temples and at wealthy tables,—
utter measures to which Lydë[3] may
    attend, though reluctant,

she who like a three-years mare on open
plains frisks playfully and shrinks from handling,
ignorant of marriage and unripe still
    for a bold husband.

You can manage woods and tigers as
companions and delay swift flowing currents;
to your blandishments the guardian of the
    horrid hall yielded,

Cérberus, although one hundred serpents
fortify his head, just like the Furies, and
reeking breath and slaver flow out of his
    triple-tongued gullet;[4]

even Títyos, yes, and Ixíon[5]
smiled unwillingly; their urns stood dry a

*Sapphic stanza*
1. Mercury (= Hermes) was the inventor of the lyre, its body made from a tortoise shell (see also Ode I.10).
2. Amphion and his brother Zethus, twin sons of Zeus and Antiope, founded Thebes, and Amphion coaxed the stones for the city's wall into place with his lyre.
3. Like the name *Lydia*, *Lyde* has voluptuous associations with the people of Asia Minor (see also Odes II.11 and III.28).
4. Some editors, including Klingner, would drop this stanza as a later addition disruptive to the flow of the poem. For Cerberus, the guardian dog of Hell, see also the last stanza of Ode II.19.
5. Tityos, for assaulting Latona (= Leto), mother of Apollo and Diana (= Artemis), had his liver plucked by two vultures and Ixion, for attempting to rape Hera, was tortured on a fiery wheel, spinning eternally.

little, while you charmed with pleasing song
Dánaüs' daughters.[6]

Of the crime let Lydë hear and of the
maidens' well-known punishment, the empty
jar with water leaking at the bottom
        and the fate, though slow,

that awaits transgressions even down in
Hades: evil—for what greater wrong could
they?—O evil who could slay with hardened
        steel their own bridegrooms.

One among the many, worthy of the
nuptial torch, was to her lying father[7]
splendidly untruthful and a maiden noble
        for all the ages:

"Wake up," she declared to her young husband,
"Wake up, lest long sleep from where you have no
fear be yours. Elude my father and my
        villainous sisters,

"who like lionesses that have taken
calves—alas—tear each apart. I am
softer: I'll not strike you nor confine you
        shut in this chamber.

"Let my father burden me with savage
chains, because in kindness I have spared my

---

6. This leads to a retelling of the myth of the fifty sons of Aegyptus, who wed
the fifty daughters of Danaus. Because of ill will towards his brother Aegyptus by
Danaus, his daughters murdered their husbands on their wedding night, except for
the noble Hypermestra, who spared her husband, Lynceus. In punishment, when
they died, the daughters of Danaus were condemned eternally to fill with water a
jar with a leaky bottom.

7. Danaus was false in arranging the marriage in the first place with malign
intentions.

piteous husband, let him banish me to
    far off Numídia:[8]

"go wherever feet and breezes take you,
    while the night and Venus favor, go with
    luck and carve upon my[9] tomb a plaintive
    memory of me."

8. Territory in North Africa around and extending west of Carthage (in modern
Tunisia and Algeria).
    9. The Latin is actually ambiguous whether it is his or her tomb that is meant.

III.12

Heartsick girls, they can neither give play to their love
nor can purge pain with wine, or are faint in their fear
of an uncle's rebuke.

Winged Love snatches your basket, Neobúlë,[1] the splendor
of Hebrus of Lípara[2] snatches your loom
and ambition to weave,

once he's washed in the Tiber his glistening shoulders,
a horseman more skilled than Bellérophon, matched
not by fist nor by foot,

who is canny at spearing stags fleeing with terrified
herds through broad fields, who is swift at confronting
a boar in dense brush.

*Ionic system*

1. The name in Greek means "one with a new plan or wish." The name appears
in early Greek literature as the young woman who rejected the Greek poet
Archilochus, who then took verbal revenge leading supposedly to Neobule's sui-
cide.

2. Hebrus is the name of a beautiful river in Thrace. N-R suggest (169) that "the
notorious chilliness of the river . . . might suggest that the young man is cold and
unresponsive." Lipara (modern Lipari) is the largest of the Aeolian Islands off the
north coast of Sicily.

III.13

Bandúsian Spring,[1] more glittering than crystal,
worthy of sweet wine along with flowers,
        tomorrow you'll receive a
            kid whose forehead swelling with

first horns portends for him both love and war—
in vain: for the offspring of the lusty
        flock will color with his
            carmine blood your icy flow.[2]

You the fierce hour of the burning Dog
Star[3] cannot touch, you offer lovely cool
        to roaming cattle and to
            oxen weary from the plow.

You too will be esteemed among the famous
springs as I tell of the oak on hollow
        rocks from which your babbling
            waters tumble down.

*Third Asclepiad system*
    1. There has been dispute whether the Bandusian Spring was located near
Horace's boyhood home in Venusia (Venosa) in southern Italy or near his Sabine
farm east of Rome. The latter appears more likely, and a prime candidate is the
handsome spring close to what is identified as Horace's Sabine villa in the Licenza
Valley.
    2. Some commentators have tried to identify the offering of the kid with a par-
ticular Roman festival, but, as N-R point out (173), "the professed occasion of the
ode is uncertain."
    3. Canicula, the Dog Star, rises on July 18.

III.14

Lately said, O Romans, to have sought for
laurels with his death,[1] like Hercules[2]
Caesar seeks again his household, back from
    Spain's shore the victor.

Let his wife,[3] rejoicing in her husband,
step forth, sacrificing to just gods,
and our brilliant leader's sister[4] and,
    adorned with thanksgiving

fillets, mothers of young maidens and the
young men lately safe; you O youths and
girls who have as yet not known a man,
    avoid words ill-omened.

Truly festival for me, this day will
drive away black cares: I will not fear
upheaval nor a violent death with Caesar
    ruling the nations.

Go, lad, look for perfumed oil and garlands
and a wine jar dating from the Marsian
war[5], if anywhere a jug's eluded
    Spartacus' plundering.[6]

---

*Sapphic stanza*
1. Augustus returned from Spain in the summer of 24 BCE, after successful
military campaigns and a bout with a grave illness, having been away for three
years.

2. N-R comment (182) that "Augustus was often compared with Hercules, the
civilizer of the world."

3 Livia Drusilla (58 BCE–29 CE), mother of the Emperor Tiberius, who married
Octavian (Augustus) in 39 BCE and was a powerful figure throughout her long life.

4. Octavia (d. 11 BCE), sister of Augustus and mother of Marcus Claudius Mar-
cellus (42–23 BCE), who until his death was a favorite of Augustus and potential
heir.

5. The Social War, Rome's war (91–87 BCE) with its Italian allies, who were seek-
ing full citizenship in the Roman state.

6. Slave revolt led by Spartacus, 73–71 BCE.

And tell dulcet-voiced Neaéra[7] to make
haste, myrrh-scented tresses tied up in a
bun: but if the hostile doorman is an
  obstacle, go off.

Hair that's turning gray makes mild a spirit
fond of arguments and reckless quarrels:
I'd not stand for this in fiery youth when
  Plancus was consul.[8]

7. N-R comment (189) that "Neaera was a name borne by *hetaerae* [courtesans],
including heroines of comedies . . . ; as the word means 'young,' it supplies a con-
trast to *albescens* [turning gray]" in the next stanza.

8. In 42 BCE, when Horace, in his early twenties, on the opposite side from
Octavian, met defeat along with Brutus and Cassius at the decisive battle of Philippi
(see also Ode II.7).

III.15


Wife of poor man Íbycus[1]
    at last put limits to your wanton ways
and infamous exertions; of
    an age not distant from the grave, give up

cavorting with the maidens and
    bestrewing fog among the shining stars.
What's well enough for Phóloë[2]
    does not become you, Chloris;[3] better she,

your daughter, storm the young men's houses,
    like a Bacchant stirred up by a drum.
Her passion for her Nothus[4] forces
    her to frolic like a lusty doe:

to spin wool shorn near famed Lucéria[5]
    is what becomes you—not the lyre
nor crimson flowers of the rose
    nor jars of wine drunk to the lees—you crone.

*Fourth Asclepiad system*
1. In looking for significance in the name *Ibycus*, two possibilities have been offered: a hedonistic sixth-century Greek lyric poet and a Pythagorean. N-R (192–93) think the latter association more convincing because of Pythagorean devotion to frugality and the likelihood that the Pythogorean Ibycus was more apt to have been a senior citizen.
2. Usually employed as the name of a girl who plays hard to get.
3. The name among other things (see on Ode II.5), can mean something like "pale-faced woman," perhaps an appropriate name for someone who is past the bloom of youth. N-R (194–95) also note that *Chloris* was the name of the mother of aged king Nestor in the *Odyssey*.
4. The name means "bastard."
5. The town in Apulia, in southern Italy, was famed for its fine wool.

III.16

A brazen tower, oaken doors, and grim
patrols of dogs on guard would have secured
imprisoned Dánaë[1] enough from gallants
    who would prowl by night,

if Jupiter and Venus had not scorned
Acrísius, the hidden maiden's fearful
keeper: "Safe and clear the pathway for
    the god become a bribe."

It's gold's delight to pass by guards and break
through rocks with greater power than a bolt
of lightning; seer Amphiaráüs' house
    collapsed and was destroyed

through lucre;[2] Macedon's King Philip[3] split
the gates of cities and upended rival
rulers with his presents; presents snare
    tough captains of the fleet.[4]

Care follows growing wealth and hunger to
have more; rightly I have trembled to
lift up my head too ostentatiously,
    Maecénas, honored knight.[5]

*Second Asclepiad system*
1. An oracle foretold that Danae, daughter of King Acrisius of Argos, would give
birth to a son who would kill her father. For this reason, Acrisius shut Danae up in
a tower of bronze, but Jupiter (= Zeus) visited her in a shower of gold and she bore
Perseus, who eventually killed Acrisius by accident.
2. Polynices bribed Eriphile, the wife of Amphiaraus, to persuade him to join the
expedition of the Seven against Thebes, in which he perished, and she in turn was
murdered by her son, Alcmeon, in revenge.
3. Philip II (382–336 BCE), king of Macedon and father of Alexander the Great,
who employed all means to win control of Greece.
4. This has been interpreted as a reference to the freedman Menas (later Meno-
dorus), who in 38 BCE deserted from the side of Sextus Pompeius to Octavian and
was generously rewarded for doing so.
5. As N-R note (206), for Maecenas, by choice a knight and not a senator, this
was "a discreet reminder that [he] Maecenas claimed to keep a low profile."

The more each one denies himself, the more
he will have from the gods: I naked seek
the camp of those not covetous and
    eagerly desert the rich,

of wealth despised more grand as master than
if I were said to hoard within my barns
all that is tilled by brisk Apúlia[6]—
    'mid great means, lacking means.

A limpid stream, a forest of few acres,
and continued trust in my own crops
—this more blessed lot eludes a magnate ruling
    fertile Africa.

Although Calabrian bees bring no honey
nor does wine from Fórmiae[7] grow mellow
in my jars nor have I lavish fleeces
    raised in Gallic fields,

still troubling poverty is far away
nor, if I should wish more, would you refuse.
Reducing my desires, I better will
    extend my slender funds

than if I join the plains of Phrygia to
the realm of Croesus. Much is wanting those
who want much: all is well for whom God grants
    enough with frugal hand.

6. A tribute to Horace's southern homeland.
7. See Ode I.20.

III.17

O Aélius,[1] ennobled by the line
of ancient Lamus[2]—since it's claimed the early
    Lámiae are named from him and
        all recorded in their archives

trace their descent from him, who, wide-ruling,
is said first to have controlled walled
    Fórmiae[3] and river Liris[4] swimming
        midst the marshes of Mintúrnae—

tomorrow, weather driven by the Southeast
Wind will scatter many leaves within
    the grove and useless seaweed on the
        shore, unless rainfall's predictor,

the long-lived crow's mistaken: while you can,
collect dry logs; tomorrow you'll relax
    with wine and suckling pig, accompanied
        by your servants freed from labor.

*Alcaic stanza*

1. Syme in *The Roman Revolution* (83 and 535; N-R, 212, concur) identifies the subject addressed as Lucius Aelius Lamia, who was Augustus's legate in Spain in 24 BCE (see also Ode I.26).

2. Lamus is mentioned in *Odyssey* X.81–82 as the mythical ruler of the Laestyrgonians' city of Telepylos, which is identified with Formiae, near where the Aelii Lamiae had an estate.

3. On the west coast of Italy between Rome and Naples and just nine miles west of the town of Minturnae.

4. A river in central Italy (today called the Garigliano in its lower reaches) flowing south and west from the Apennines and emptying into the Tyrrhenian Sea.

III.18

Faunus,[1] lover of the nymphs who flee you,
through the boundaries of my sunny farm may
you walk gently and depart propitious
      to the small nurslings,

if a tender kid is offered at year's
end, wine's abundant in the crater,
friend of Venus, and the ancient altar
      smokes with much incense.

All the flock is playing on the grassy
field, when your day December fifth[2]
returns; in the meadows country folk and
      oxen are at ease;

with emboldened lambs the wolf is straying,
rustic leaves for you the forest scatters,
triple steps of joy the digger pounds
      upon the earth, his foe.

*Sapphic stanza*

1. A Roman god of the forests and protector of flocks, identified with the Greek
god Pan.

2. The date of the Faunalia, honoring Faunus as protector of the flocks.

III.19

How far in time was Ínachus
    from Codrus[1] unafraid to die for country—
that's your theme and Aéacus's
    family[2] and the wars at holy Troy:

at what price we may buy a jar
    of Chian vintage,[3] who will heat the water,[4]
who provide the house, what hour
    I may escape harsh cold, you do not say.

Quick, pour to mark the new moon, lad,[5]
    to honor midnight, and to celebrate
Muréna[6] made an augur: cups
    be mixed with brimming ladles—three or nine.

The bard, who loves the Muses nine,
    inspired will ask for ladles three times three;
one of the Graces,[7] naked sisters arm
    in arm, in fear of brawls, forbids that we

touch more than three: our pleasure is
    in madness: why do Berecýnthian
pipes[8] cease blowing? Why is it
    the panpipe hangs in silence with the lyre?

*Fourth Asclepiad system*
    1. Inachus was the first king of Argos, and Codrus was the last king of Athens, sacrificing himself to save the city from the invading Dorians.
    2. Aeacus was father of Peleus and grandfather of Achilles.
    3. The island of Chios in the eastern Aegean was famed in antiquity for its wine.
    4. The water is heated to be mixed with wine.
    5. Addressed to a servant. ,
    6. Usually identified with the outspoken Licinius Murena (the Licinius in Ode II.10), brother-in-law of Maecenas and consul in 23 BCE, who was removed from office and then implicated in a conspiracy against Augustus. He was put to death after trying to escape. N-R suggest (227) the brother of this Murena or Aulus Terentius Varro Murena, consul elect in 23 BCE.
    7. The three minor goddesses, the Graces, personified charm, grace, and beauty.
    8. The Berecyntes were a Phrygian tribe, so the adjective is a poetic way of saying "Phrygian." These flutes were originally associated with the goddess Cybele, who originated in Asia Minor.

I hate right hands closefisted: scatter
   roses: let the jealous Lycus[9] and
our neighbor lady, who's not suited
   to old Lycus, hear the crazy din.

You with thick, glist'ning head of hair,
   you, Télephus,[10] who're like the shining Evening
Star, the blooming Rhodë[11] seeks:
   my smould'ring love for Glýcera[12] sears me.

---

9. Greek for "wolf."

10. N-R (238) comment that in connection with the reference to the Evening Star, which is the planet Venus, "the name Telephus may have suggested 'shining far,'" from the Greek words *tēle* (far) and *phōs* (light).

11. "Rose bush," a name that N-R (238) see as likely to belong to a courtesan.

12. "Sweet woman" (see Ode I.33).

III.20

Don't you see at what great danger, Pyrrhus,[1]
you disturb the Moorish lioness's
cubs? Shy robber, very soon you'll flee a
    difficult battle,

when among the thronging group of youths she'll
come to claim again the fair Neárchus[2]—
a huge contest whether greater prize will
    fall to you or her.[3]

Meantime, while you ready nimble arrows,
while she sharpens terrifying fangs, the
battle's judge is said to put the victor's
    palm 'neath his bare foot

and amidst a gentle breeze refresh his
shoulders sprinkled with his scented hair, like
Nireus[4] or the boy[5] who was borne off from
    well-watered Ida.

*Sapphic stanza*
1. The name *Pyrrhus*, from the Greek word for fire (*pur*), means "male with reddish-blond or auburn hair." *Pyrrhus* is, of course, the name of the Hellenistic king of Epirus, whose costly victories made his name a byword for success at an excessive cost. This may be behind Horace's use of the name here, especially with the hunting imagery.
2. The name means appropriately "leader of the youth" in this context, according to N-R (242).
3. The "greater prize" has been interpreted to mean the greater sexual satisfaction from Nearchus. The passage has also been emended so that it reads "a huge contest whether the prize be yours or / she will be stronger," but N-R (242) object that such an interpretation, even with the emendation, would require a strained reading of the syntax.
4. Fairest Greek warrior at Troy after Achilles.
5. The handsome young Trojan prince Ganymede was carried off by Zeus from Mount Ida to Mount Olympus to be cupbearer to the gods.

III.21

O born the same as I when Manlius
was consul,[1] whether you bring on complaints
    or jokes or brawls or maddened love or,
        dutiful jar, easy slumber,

whatever reason you preserve choice Massic
vintage,[2] worthy to be brought out on
    a special day, descend, since
        Messálla[3] orders wines more mellow.

Though he is steeped in dialogues Socratic,
he will not neglect you churlishly:
    it's said that even ancient Cato's[4]
        virtue often warmed with drinking.

You offer gentle spur to those who would
be guarded, you uncover worries of
    the wise and secret counsels to the
        genial Emancipator,[5]

you bring back hope to troubled spirits and
add strength and courage to the poor man: after

---

*Alcaic stanza*
1. Lucius Manlius Torquatus was consul in 65 BCE.
2. A fine wine from fertile Mount Massicus in the Campania in west-central Italy north of Naples.
3. Marcus Valerius Messalla Corvinus (64 BCE–8 CE) was a Roman patrician who originally fought on the side of Brutus and Cassius but, after their defeat at Philippi in 42 BCE, first sided with Antony and then Octavian. He was a noted orator and a great patron of poetry, supporting Tibullus, Ovid, Lygdamus, and his own niece Sulpicia.
4. Marcus Porcius Cato (234–149 BCE), leading politician and literary figure of his day, was devoted to old-fashioned Roman values.
5. Translation of the Latinized Greek cult title of Dionysus/Bacchus, *Lyaeus*.

you he does not fear the angry
  crowns of kings nor soldiers' weapons.

You're led by Liber[6] and gay Venus, if
she's present, and the Graces[7] slow to loose
  their bond and lamps ablaze, until
    returning Phoebus[8] routs the stars.

6. Latin rural fertility deity identified with Dionysus.
7. The three minor goddesses, the Graces, arm in arm, personified charm, grace, and beauty. The "bond" has been interpreted as their linked arms or the cinctures of their clothing.
8. Epithet of Apollo as sun god, meaning "pure, bright, radiant."

III.22

Virgin guardian of groves and mountains,[1]
you who, called three times,[2] attend and keep from
death young women laboring in childbirth,
        goddess in three forms,[3]

let the pine that overhangs my farmhouse
be yours, which with joy each year I may
present with blood of a young boar still practicing
        blows struck sidelong.[4]

*Sapphic stanza*
1. This hymn is addressed to Diana.
2. Three is a ritually significant number.
3. On earth she is Diana (= Artemis), goddess of woodlands and wild nature,
and in her Greek form as Artemis presides over fertility and childbirth; in the heav-
ens she is Luna (= Selene in Greek), the moon goddess; and in the Underworld, as
Hecate, with Persephone she presides over the dead and is associated with magic
and sorcery.
4. Quinn notes (281) that the dedication of the pine tree is in recognition of her
connection to woodlands, and the boar recalls her role as goddess of the hunt.

III.23

If you will raise your hands upturned to heaven,
with the new Moon, rustic Phídyle,[1]
    if you appease the Larës[2] with a
        fat sow, this year's grain, and incense,[3]

the fruitful vine will not know the pernicious
Southwest Wind nor wheat crops barren blight
    nor charming nurslings burdensome
        weather during apple harvest.

The consecrated victim grazing snowy
Álgidus[4] among the oaks and
    ilexes or on the grasses of the
        Alban Hills will with its neck stain

the pontiffs' axes;[5] it is not at all
for you, who crown your little gods with
    rosemary and fragile myrtle, to
        approach them with many sheep slaughtered.

If giftless hands have touched an altar, where
they're not more welcome by rich sacrifice,
    they've softened hostile household gods with
        grain and salt[6] devoutly offered.

*Alcaic stanza*
1. The name, from the Greek verb *pheidomai* (to spare, be thrifty), means "thrifty woman."
2. Guardian spirits of the house and household.
3. All three of these, even the sow, are inexpensive sacrifices.
4. Mountain in the Alban Hills in Latium southeast of Rome.
5. The pontiffs were Rome's most important college of priests, their leading member, the *pontifex maximus*, being the chief priest of the state.
6. Grain and salt are symbolic, token offerings, which normally would accompany an actual sacrifice.

III.24

More wealthy than the untouched
    treasuries of Araby and India,
though you with your constructions
    occupy all lands along the Tuscan shore,

if dread Necessity drives its
    unyielding spikes into the highest vault,
you will not extricate your heart
    from fear nor free your head from snares of death.

The Scythians of the plains, whose carts,
    as is their custom, drag their wandering homes,
live better, and the rugged Getae[1]
    too, for whom unmeasured acres bear

free fruits and cereals; nor do
    they please to till fields longer than a year,
and then another man succeeds
    refreshing him whose term of work is done.

And there a blameless wife treats with
    forbearance stepchildren without a mother
and no dowered spouse controls
    her mate or trusts a polished paramour.

For virtue's the great dowry of
    their parents and a purity within
the marriage bond that fears another
    man: to stray is wrong—the price is death.

Whoever wishes to remove
    unpatriotic gore and civic rage,
if he will be inscribed on statues
    "Father of our Cities," let him dare

*Fourth Asclepiad system*
1. Thracian tribe living on the lower Danube.

to curb untamed licentiousness,
    by future generations loved—O wrong!—
since jealous we hate virtue that's
    alive and long for it when not in sight.

What good are sorrowful complaints,
    if sin is not pruned back by punishment?
What good are empty laws without
    Morality, if neither that part of

the world enclosed by burning heat
    nor places nearest to the North Wind nor
the snows hard frozen on the ground
    drive off the merchant, if skilled sailors best

tumultuous seas, if Poverty,
    the cause of huge reproach, commands one to
endure and take on anything
    and to abandon virtue's lofty path?

Let us consign our gems and pearls
    and useless gold, the source of greatest evil,
either to the Capitol,[2]
    where shouts of crowds proclaim approval or

consign them to the nearby sea,
    if we are deeply sorry for our crimes.
The elements of warped desire
    must be rooted out and spirits over-

delicate be firmed by training
    more severe. The unskilled, well-born boy
does not know how to sit a horse
    and fears to hunt, more informed at games,

if you should bid him whirl Greek hoops
    or play at dice forbidden by our laws,

2. To the temple of Jupiter on the Capitoline Hill, i.e., to the state.

while his mendacious father's pledge
  deceives his business partner and his guests

and hurries after money for
  his worthless heir. Yes, it is clear: dishonest
wealth proliferates: none-
  theless, it's always somehow incomplete.

III.25

Where do you take me, Bacchus,[1] filled
   with you? To what groves or what grottoes am
I borne, swift in my mind made new?
   In what caves will I be heard trying to

insert great Caesar's lasting glory
   midst the stars and at Jove's counsels? I
will sing of something notable,
   fresh, still unspoken by another. As

a sleepless Maenad on the heights
   is stunned when looking at the Hebrus[2] and
Thrace white with snow and Rhódopë[3]
   traversed by strangers, so for me beyond

the beaten track it pleases to
   admire the river banks and lonely grove.
Ruler of Naiads and of Bacchants
   able to uproot with hands tall ash,

I'll speak of nothing small or in
   a lowly style, nothing mortal. O
Lenaéus,[4] sweet the danger to
   attend a god, brows tied with tendrils green.[5]

*Fourth Asclepiad system*
1. In this poem, Dionysus/Bacchus is god of poetry and poetic inspiration.
2. The major river in eastern Thrace at the boundary between Greece and Turkey,
today called the Evros, or Maritza.
3. The major mountain range in Thrace.
4. A title of Dionysus, derived from *lênê*, meaning Maenad.
5. This phrase "brows tied with tendrils green" can be read in the Latin to refer
either to the god or to the poet, N-R (308–9) inclining to the latter.

III.26

I recently lived suitable to ladies,
and I played the soldier not without glory:
    now my weapons and my lyre
        discharged from service will be hung on

this wall, which guards the left side of the shrine
of sea-born Venus: here, here put the glowing
    torches, crowbars, and the axes,
        that are threats to doors opposing.

O goddess,[1] you who dwell in blessèd Cyprus
and in Memphis lacking Thracian snows,
    O queen, with lash raised high, flick just
        once the arrogant Chloë![2]

*Alcaic stanza*

As N-R point out (309–10) the poem includes the motifs of a sepulchral inscrip-
tion, a dedicatory inscription, the locked-out lover's serenade (*paraklausithyron*, cf.
Ode III.10), and the theme of the renunciation of amorous pursuits, all of which
are common in both Greek and Latin poetry.

   1. Venus.

   2. The name means "the first green shoot of plants" in spring and suggests
freshness and immaturity.

III.27

Let a calling owl's omen and a
pregnant bitch or tawny she-wolf running
from Lanúvium[1] or gravid vixen
    escort the wicked;

let a serpent interrupt their journey,
if it, sidelong like an arrow, terrifies
their ponies. I, farsighted seer to
    her for whom I will

worry, I will rouse with prayers an augur
raven's cry where first the sun appears, before
that prophet bird of threatening rain seeks
    stagnant swamps once more.

Happy may you be, wherever you wish,
and be mindful of me, Galatéa,[2]
nor may an ill-omened woodpecker or
    wandering crow stop you.

But do you observe with what turmoil
Oríon[3] rushes headlong? I know what the
inky Adriatic's like and of the
    clear West Wind's mischief.

Let the wives and children of our foes
experience blind raging of the rising
South Wind and the rumbling of black seas and
    the surf-lashed shoreline.

*Sapphic stanza*
    This ode is a *propempticon*, a poem wishing a prosperous journey. The poet
begins with a series of omens unlucky for the wicked.
    1. A city in the Alban Hills, twenty miles southeast of Rome.
    2. *Galatea* likely means "milk-white," and is the name of a nymph once pursued
by the Cyclops Polyphemus.
    3. Orion sets in early November.

It was thus Europa[4] once entrusted
to the crafty bull her snow-white body,
and, though daring, blanched at waters thronged with
    monsters and peril.

Recently in meadows hunting flowers
and creating garlands promised to the
Nymphs, in glimm'ring darkness she saw nothing
    but waves and starlight.

On her reaching Crete great with one hundred
cities, she said: "Father—O abandoned
is the name of daughter[5] and my duty
    conquered by madness!

"From where, to where have I come? One death is
trifling for a maiden's sin. Awake do
I lament a vile offense or blameless
    does a vain vision

"mock me, which escaping from the ivory
gate brings on a dream?[6] Was it better
to traverse amid the far waves or to
    gather fresh flowers?

"If they'd give me, now while angry, that
disgraceful bull, I would try to maim and
smash with steel the horns of that so recently
    much-loved monster.

"Shameless I deserted my own household:
shameless I delay descent to Hades.

4. The daughter of King Agenor (or Phoenix) of Tyre was loved by Jupiter
(= Zeus), who enticed her by taking the form of a beautiful bull and then carried
her over the sea to Crete.

5. N-R (329–30) interpret the beginning of Europa's outburst to mean "Father, O
name abandoned by your daughter," *filiae* (daughter) being translated as a dative of
agent rather than as a genitive of possession.

6. In *Odyssey* XIX.562–67, Penelope explains that dreams that issue from a gate
of ivory are false, while dreams from a gate of horn are true.

O gods, if you hear this, may I wander
    naked with lions;

"I desire to nourish tigers, while still
beautiful, before vile leanness furrows
these fair cheeks and the juice of this tender
    quarry has dried up."

"'Base Europa, why delay to die?' your
far-off father urges. 'With your maiden's
girdle happily at hand, you can
    hang from this ash tree.

"'Or if cliffs and boulders sharp with death
delight you, come entrust yourself to rushing
wind, unless, of royal blood, you
    prefer to spin wool in

"'servitude and as a concubine be
at the mercy of a foreign mistress.'"
Venus with sly smile was near and her
    son, his bow unstrung.

Soon when she had had her fun, she said to
her: "Keep from anger and from quarrels,
when the hated bull will bring you back his
    horns for your maiming.

How to be the wife of matchless Jove you
do not fathom: stop sobbing: learn to
bear great fortune well: one half the world from
    you will take its name."

## III.28

What better might I do on Neptune's
    festival?[1] Quickly, Lydë,[2] bring out
the laid up Caécuban[3] and launch
    assaults on fortified sobriety.

You sense it's now past noontime and,
    as if the swift day would stand still, do you
forgo to snatch from stores the jar
    that's lingered since the days of Bíbulus?[4]

We taking turns will sing of Neptune
    and the green hair of the Néreïds:[5]
with the curved lyre you will hymn
    Latóna[6] and the darts of fleet Diana.

Last a song for her[7] who rules
    in Cnidus and the shining Cýclades,
who visits Paphos with her team
    of swans; and Night will rate a lullaby.

*Fourth Asclepiadic system*
1. The Neptunalia, on July 23, when Neptune was especially honored because of
the naval victories of Augustus over Pompey's son Sextus in 36 BCE and Antony
and Cleopatra at the Battle of Actium in 31 BCE.
2. Like the name *Lydia, Lyde* has voluptuous associations with the people of Asia
Minor (see also Odes II.11 and III.11).
3. A fine vintage (see Ode I.20).
4. Marcus Cornelius Bibulus was consul in 59 BCE; the pun seems intended.
5. Sea goddesses, the daughters of the sea god Nereus, their hair the color of
seaweed.
6. Mother of Apollo and Diana (= Artemis).
7. Venus.

## III.29

Descendant of Etruscan kings, for you,
Maecénas, mellow wine sealed in a never-
    opened jar has long been in my
        stores, with flowers of the rose and

pressed balsam to perfume your hair. Put off
delay, do not be always gazing out
    at Túsculum and Aéfula's sloped
        meadows and well-watered Tibur.[1]

Abandon tiresome abundance and
your mansion, neighbor to the lofty clouds,
    and leave admiring the smoke and
        wealth and noise of Rome the blessèd.

Quite often change is pleasing to the rich
and graceful meals within a poor man's home,
    without the tapestries of purple
        thread, have evened brows of worry.

Now in July bright Cepheus shows his hidden
fire, now Prócyon is raging and
    the star of maddened Leo,[2] as the
        sun brings back days parched and withered;

now with his listless flock the weary shepherd
seeks a stream and shade and scrubby thickets
    of Silvánus,[3] and the silent
        river bank receives no breezes:

*Alcaic stanza*
  1. These towns in Latium make an arc around Rome, beginning in the south.
Tusculum is southeast of Rome and Aefula farther to the northeast, between Prae-
neste and Tibur, and Tibur still further to the northeast, on the Anio at the border
of Sabine country, not too far from Horace's farm. The order is reversed from the
original Latin, which begins with Tibur in the north.
  2. The constellation Cepheus, Procyon ("Fore Dog" in Greek), the major star in
Canis Minor, and the brightest star of the constellation Leo, the *stella regia*, all rise
in July.
  3. Italian god of the woodlands, often identified with the Greek god Pan.

you worry what arrangement suits the state
and anxious for the City are afraid
    of what the Chinese, Persians, and the
        restless Scythians are planning.

God wisely covers in the mists of night
the consequence of future times and laughs
    if mortal man is vexed beyond what
        is allowed. Remember, handle

with poise what is at hand: like a stream
the rest is born along, now in mid-channel
    flowing peacefully to the
        Etruscan Sea,⁴ now churning with it

eroded rocks and stumps wrenched up and homes
and cattle, not without an echo in
    the mountains and the neighboring forests,
        when the savage deluge roils

calm waters. Self-possessed and happy he
will be, who can declare each day "I've lived."
    Tomorrow let our father Jove
        embrace the heavens with black clouds or

with shining sun: he nonetheless will not
annul whatever now is past nor will
    he alter and undo that which the
        fleeing hour once has taken.

Fortúna, happy in her ruthless business,
stubborn in her playing on surprise,
    transfers uncertain honors, now to
        me, now to another, gracious.

I praise her when she stays: if she beats
swift wings, I yield her gifts, I wrap myself
    in my own courage, and I seek an
        honest poverty undowered.

4. Tyrrhenian Sea.

It's not my way, if masts should groan in storms
from Africa, to run to wretched prayers
   and to negotiate through vows lest
      wares from Cyprus and from Tyre

should add to riches in the greedy sea:
at that time breezes and twin Pollux[5] will
   convey me safely in my two-oared
      rowboat through Aegean tempests.

5. The Dioscuri, "sons of Zeus," the twins Pollux and Castor, watched over
sailors.

III.30

I have achieved a monument more
permanent than bronze and higher than the royal
pyramids, which no devouring rain,
no raging North Wind can destroy or years

in endless series or the flight of time.
I will not wholly die; much will escape
the Goddess of the Dead:[1] through future praise
I will grow ever fresh, while yet a priest

with silent Vestal climbs the Capitol.[2]
I will be mentioned, where the wild
Aúfidus resounds, where Daunus,[3] poor
in water, governed rustic peoples, as

the one, although of humble birth, able
first to bring Aeólic song to Latin
verse. Justly proud, Melpómene,[4]
with Delphic laurel gladly wreathe my hair.

*First Asclepiad system*

This poem, completing the first three books of the *Odes* published together in 23 BCE, is in the same meter as Ode I.1.

1. In the Latin, *Libitina,* who presided over burials.
2. Capitoline Hill in Rome, where the principal temple to Jupiter was located.
3. The Aufidus is a river in Apulia emptying into the Adriatic, not far from Horace's birthplace, Venusia (Venosa); Daunus was a mythical king of Apulia.
4. Muse whose name means "songstress."

# BOOK IV

IV.1

Once more do you rouse wars long
    discontinued, Venus? Spare, spare me, I pray.
I am not what I was when kindly
    Cínara[1] held sway. Cruel mother of

desires sweet, have done with bending one
    who, reaching fifty years, now is hardened
to your soft commands; go off
    to where youths' coaxing prayers call you back.

More seasonably you on wings
    of purple swans will pass with revels to
the house of Paullus Maximus,[2]
    if you intend to scorch a fitting heart.

For he both wellborn and fair favored,
    eloquent for those accused and troubled,
young man of a hundred skills,
    will bear your standards widely on campaign,

and when he's laughed victorious
    against a lavish rival's presents, near
the Alban lakes[3] he'll raise for you
    a marble statue under citron beams.

There you'll inhale abundant incense
    and will be delighted by the lyre

*Fourth Asclepliad system*
1. An earlier love of Horace, also referred to in Ode IV.13 and Epistles I.7 and 14.
2. Paullus Fabius Maximus, consul in 11 BCE, was a close friend of Augustus.
3. The Alban Lake and Lake Nemi, about twelve miles southeast of Rome.

and the Berecýnthic flute[4]
in songs that also blend the shepherd's pipe.

There twice a day young men with tender
maidens praising your divinity
will shake the earth three times with bare
feet flashing like the leaping Salii.[5]

A woman or a boy or hope
of love that is returned is not
my pleasure now nor drinking contests
nor to bind my temples with fresh blooms.

But why, ah Ligurínus,[6] why
do scattered tears slip down along my checks?
Why in mid-sentence does my fertile
tongue fall to unseemly speechlessness?

In dreams at night I hold you now
within my arms, now follow you fleet-footed
through the grasses of the Field
of Mars,[7] through waters, moving on, hard lad.

4. The Berecyntes were a Phrygian tribe, so the adjective is a poetic way of saying
"Phrygian." These flutes were originally associated with the goddess Cybele, who
originated in Asia Minor.
5. The priests of Mars, the Salii, dressed in armor, and each carried a figure-eight
shield called an *ancile*. Their name derived from their leaping ritual dance (from
the verb *salio*, "to leap").
6. The name means Ligurian, a member of a Celtic tribe in northern Italy—a
slave or freedman's name.
7. *Campus Martius* in Latin, the Tiber flood plain on the northwest side of Rome,
which, during the republic, was used as an exercise ground, meeting area, and vot-
ing place but gradually was built up, especially during the empire.

IV.2

Anyone who tries to rival Pindar,
Jullus,[1] counts on wings wax-fastened through the
skill of Daédalus—to offer to the
 glitt'ring sea his name.[2]

Like a river running down a mountain,
which the rains have swelled beyond its known banks,
Pindar seethes and rushes on immense in
 depth of expression,

worthy of the laurel of Apollo,[3]
whether in audacious dithyrambs he
pours forth new words and is borne along in
 verse free in meter,

or he sings of gods or kings born of the
blood of gods, by whom the Centaurs justly
were laid low, by whom the dread hot-breathed
 Chimaéra[4] was laid low,

or if he extols the boxer or the
racehorse, honored winners of Olympic
glory, and bestows a better gift than
 one hundred statues,

or if he laments a youth wrenched from his
weeping bride and raises to the stars his

*Sapphic stanza*
1. Jullus Antonius, son of Mark Antony, was author of a poem on the epic hero Diomedes.
2. The ingenious craftsman and inventor Daedalus, accompanied by his son Icarus, escaped imprisonment in Crete by creating wings fastened with wax, but when Icarus passed too near the sun, the wax binding his wings melted, and he fell to his death in a part of the Aegean which then came to be called the Sea of Icarus.
3. In this and the next three stanzas, Horace summarized the various types of poetry that brought fame to the great choral poet Pindar of Thebes (518–after 446 BCE): the metrically bold dithyrambs dedicated to Dionysus, paeans to Apollo and hymns celebrating other gods, victory songs for athletes successful in the great games of Greece (which alone have survived complete), and dirges for the dead.
4. The monster with the head of a lion, body of a goat, and tail of a snake was slain by Bellerophon riding the winged horse Pegasus.

strength, his spirit, and his golden ways and
    grudges black Hades.

Huge the breeze that lifts the Theban swan,
Antonius, as often as he reaches
for the high expanse of clouds; I, like the
    Matine[5] bee that goes

gathering enticing thyme by mighty
effort, round the groves and banks of Tibur[6]
rich in waters, small in size, I shape my
    painstaking poems.

You a poet of more breadth will sing of
Caesar, when, adorned with well-earned laurel,
he will lead along the Sacred Way[7] the
    fiercesome Sygámbri.[8]

Nothing greater, nothing better here
upon this earth have fate and kind gods given
nor will give, even if a golden
    age should come once more;

you will sing of joyful days and of the
city's public games to honor brave
Augustus's longed-for return and of the
    law courts in recess.[9]

Then my voice, if I may speak words worth a
hearing, in good measure will join in and
"O fair sun, O praised," I'll sing with joy now
    Caesar has come home.

---

    5. Name of an unidentified geographic location in southern Italy, perhaps near
Tarentum.
    6. Resort town, east of Rome on the Anio river on the border between Latium
and Sabine territory.
    7. The major street in Rome, which goes through the Forum, and along which all
triumphal processions would pass.
    8. A Germanic tribe.
    9. During public holidays, the activities of the courts were suspended.

And you while you take the lead, "O triumph,"
we will cry repeatedly, "O triumph,"
all the citizens, and to the gracious
    gods offer incense.

Ten bulls and as many cows will free you,
me a tender calf, who after he has
left his mother, grows on ample grass to
    satisfy my vows,

imitating with a mark of snowy
white upon his brow curved fires of the
moon on its third rising, all the rest of
    him being tawny.

IV.3

Whom you have contemplated once
   at birth with peaceful eye, Melpómene,[1]
no Isthmian exertions[2] will
   bring glory as a boxer, no unflagging

steed will lead him victor in
   a Grecian chariot nor warfare show
him leader graced with laurels on
   the Capitol,[3] because he has demolished

the inflated threats of kings;
   but waters which flow past productive Tibur
and lush foliage of its groves
   will shape him honored for Aeólic song.

The progeny of Rome, the queen
   of cities, deems me worthy to include
among its favored choirs of bards
   and now I'm bitten less by Envy's tooth.

O Muse, you who modulate
   the golden tortoise shell's sweet thrumming,[4] you
who also may confer on voiceless
   fish, if it should please, the song of swans,

all this exists a gift from you:
   that I am pointed out by passersby
the player of the Roman lyre;
   that I'm inspired and may appeal is yours.

---

*Fourth Asclepiad system*

1. Muse whose name means "songstress."
2. The Isthmian Games, one of the four major athletic festivals of Greece, were held at the precinct of Poseidon (= Neptune) on the isthmus between Central Greece and the Peloponnese.
3. Location of the major temple of Jupiter in Rome, where triumphal processions would end.
4. Tortoise shells were used for the bowl in constructing a lyre.

IV.4

Just like the eagle, keeper of the thunder-
bolt, whom Jupiter gave kingship over
    roving birds—having found him
        true when Gánymede[1] was taken—

whose youth and innate energy first pushed
him from the nest, still unaware of struggles;
    then in cloudless skies the winds of
        springtime taught him, though still fearful,

untried endeavors; soon a lively thrust
dispatched him down a foe against the sheepfolds;
    now love of feast and battle drove him
        on against defiant serpents;

or like the lion, banished from his tawny
mother's milk, whom a roe-deer, while
    intent on lush grasses, has sighted
        when about to be devoured:

so the Vindélici have sighted Drusus[2]
waging war below the Raetian Alps;
    (from where their age-old custom comes to
        arm their right hands with the axes

of Amazons, I defer to ask
nor is it lawful to know all)[3] but bands
    long conquering far and wide in turn were
        conquered through a young man's judgment,

---

*Alcaic stanza*
    1. In one version of the story, the handsome young Trojan prince Ganymede was
carried off by Zeus in the form of an eagle from Mount Ida to Mount Olympus to
become cupbearer to the gods.
    2. Nero Claudius Drusus, son of Livia, wife of Augustus, and younger brother of
Tiberius Claudius Nero, the future emperor Tiberius, fought the Celtic-Illyrian Vin-
delici in Raetia, which includes the Tyrol and part of Bavaria and Switzerland.
    3. This and the three lines preceding are sometimes bracketed as a later inser-
tion, but some have regarded them as imparting a certain Pindaric quality in this
very Pindaric poem.

and they perceived what mind, what character
well nurtured in a favored household, what
    Augustus's affection for the
        young Nerónes[4] could accomplish.

The brave are born of those both brave and good;
in bullocks, in young horses is the courage
    of their fathers nor are warless
        doves begotten by fierce eagles.

But education fosters inborn strength
and proper training fortifies the heart;
    whenever morals are deficient,
        faults dishonor native merit.

O Rome, what you owe to the Nerónes,[5]
the Metaúrus River testifies
    and Hásdrubal defeated and that fair
        day for Latium, which, when darkness

fled, smiled the first with nurturing acclaim,
since the dread African had ridden through
    Italian towns, like flame through pines or
        East Wind through Sicilian waters.[6]

From then on Roman youth advanced in ever
prosp'rous efforts and shrines devastated
    by the wicked Punic onset
        held their gods now standing upright,

and faithless Hannibal at last declared:
"Though deer, prey of voracious wolves, still we
    chase after those it is abundant
        triumph to elude and flee from.

4. The plural of Nero and referring to Drusus and Tiberius. Putnam (90–91)
points out that the word *nero* in the Sabine language means "brave."
    5. The whole line of the Claudii Nerones.
    6. The defeat in 207 BCE of Hannibal's brother Hasdrubal at the Metaurus River
by Marcus Livius Salinator and Gaius Claudius Nero, the latter, an ancestor of the
Nerones of the poem. This battle is usually regarded as decisive in turning the Sec-
ond Punic War in Rome's favor.

"That people, who from ravaged Ílium,
   tossed on the Tuscan sea,[7] bravely brought
      their gods, their children, and their agèd
         fathers to Ausónian[8] cities,

"just like the holm oak pruned by sturdy axes
   on Mount Álgidus[9] rich with dark leaves,
      through blows, through losses from the very
         iron draws resource and courage.

"The Hydra, with its body cut, did not
   grow stronger battling shaken Hercules[10]
      nor did the Colchians raise a greater
         monster nor the Thebes of Cadmus.[11]

"Sink them in the depths, fairer they come forth;
   contend with them, with ample praise they will
      cast down the unscathed victor and wage
         battles for their wives to boast of.

"No longer will I send to Carthage vaunting
   messages: all hope and fortune in
      our name have now collapsed, collapsed since
         Hásdrubal has been struck down."[12]

There's nothing that the Claudii[13] will not
   achieve whom Jove protects with favoring
      power and astute attention
         extricates mid warfare's crises.

7. Tyrrhenian Sea.
8. Poetic name for the inhabitants of Italy.
9. In the Alban Hills in Latium southeast of Rome.
10. To Hercules' dismay, the many-headed water snake Hydra grew new heads as soon as the hero cut them off.
11. Jason on his quest for the Golden Fleece in Colchis had to yoke fire-breathing bulls and slay warriors that grew from the teeth of a dragon once slain by the Theban hero Cadmus, who himself had had to confront warriors sown from the teeth of that same dragon.
12. Quinn and SB end Hannibal's speech here, while K extends it to the final stanza.
13. The Nerones.

IV.5

Descended of kind gods, best guardian
of the Roman people, you're away
too long: a swift return you promised to
      the Senate: now return!

Restore light to your country, kindly leader.
For like spring, when your face shines upon
your people, days go by more pleasingly,
      more brightly gleams the sun.

Just as the mother of a youth, whom
the spiteful South Wind's blowing keeps delayed
across the east Aegean longer than
      a year from his sweet home,

addresses him with vows and prayers and omens
and does not stop from looking at the curving
shore, so his country longs for Caesar
      with a staunch desire.

For cattle safely walk the countryside,
the countryside that fostering abundance
nurtures; sailors speed through peaceful seas;
      a broken pledge fears blame;

chaste homes are fouled by no disgrace; tradition
and the law have conquered evil's stain;
there's praise for women pregnant by their husbands;
      punishment quells sin.

Who fears the Parthians, the Scythians
of freezing climes or those the German
forests spawn, while Caesar's safe? Who thinks
      of wars in wild Spain?

*Second Asclepiad system*

Each brings the day to close in his own hills
and to the waiting tree unites the vine;[1]
then joyful home again, invites you to
    his table as a god.[2]

With many prayers, with wine in offering poured,
he honors you and with his Larës[3] mixes
your divinity, as Greece hails Castor
    and great Hercules.

"O may you grant unto Hespéria,[4]
kind leader, lengthy festivals," we sober
say when day is new, and tippling say
    when Ocean holds the sun.

1. In ancient viticulture, vines were trained to be supported by trees.
2. Quinn comments (309) that though "worship of the living Augustus as a god was officially frowned upon, . . . [Cassius] Dio 51.19 records . . . that in 24 BC the Senate decreed that libations could be poured to Augustus in both private and public banquets."
3. Guardian spirits of the house and household.
4. Greek for "Western Land" = Italy.

## IV.6

God, by whom the seed of Níobë met
vengeance for her boastful tongue and rapist
Títyos and almost victor over high Troy
    Phthian Achilles,[1]

he a soldier greater than the rest, but
not your equal, though as son of sea-born
Thetis with dread spear he made the Dardan[2]
    battlements tremble—

he, just like a pine struck by a biting
blade or cypress pounded by the East Wind,
tumbled prostrate and he laid his neck in
    the dust of Ílion;

he would not, enclosed within the horse that
feigned an offering to Minerva, trick the
wrongly reveling Trojans and the joyful
    palace of Priam,

but in open battle cruel to captives—
O unspeakable—he'd burn in Grecian
fires infants, even hiding in the
    wombs of their mothers,

had the Father of the Gods, convinced by
you and pleasing Venus, not assented
to Aeneas' fortune that with better
    omens walls be traced:[3]

*Sapphic stanza*
   1. Niobe with six or seven children of each sex claimed superiority to Latona
(= Leto) who only had two children, Apollo and Diana (= Artemis). For this pre-
sumptuous boast, Apollo and Diana slew her children and Niobe in her grief was
turned into a stone on Mount Sipylus in Lydia. Tityus, a Giant, while attempting to
rape Latona, was slain by Apollo and Diana. Achilles, whose home was Phthia in
Thessaly, at the end of the Trojan War was brought down by an arrow of Paris, with
the aid of Apollo.
   2. Trojan.
   3. Had Achilles lived, he might have annihilated all the Trojans including
Aeneas, who escaped to Italy to become the ancestor of Rome's founder, Romulus.

lyre-playing teacher of clear-singing
Thalia,[4] Phoebus, you who in the river
Xanthus[5] bathe your hair, protect the grace of
    the Muse of Daunus.[6]

[7]Phoebus gave me inspiration, gave me
skill in verse-craft and the name of poet:
noble maidens and young men born of
    illustrious fathers,

under Delian Diana's care, who
with her bow stops fleeing deer and lynxes,[8]
mark the Sapphic measure and the rhythm
    struck on my lyre,

as you celebrate Latóna's son
and the shining Moon[9] with waxing torch,
promoting harvests and at speed to cycle
    headlong round the months.

When a married woman, you'll say: "At the
Festival Centennial,[10] I
performed a song that pleased the gods, trained in
    verse of bard Horace."

---

4. A Muse, her name means "abundance."

5. Phoebus (= Apollo). The river Xanthus is in Lycia in southwest Asia Minor, near which was a famous sanctuary of Apollo's mother Latona (= Leto).

6. Mythical king of Apulia, birthplace of Horace.

7. As SB observes, some would see a new poem starting at this point.

8. Quinn notes (311) that "the appositional expansion ["who with her bow stops fleeing deer and lynxes"] . . . identifies Diana as the huntress goddess . . . , always represented as fiercely chaste, and the protectress, therefore, of the young and chaste."

9. Diana, who is the goddess of wild nature, is considered a moon goddess similar to the way her brother Apollo, especially as Phoebus, "the bright one," is identified with the sun.

10. The *Ludi Saeculares* (Centennial Games) were celebrated by the Emperor Augustus from 31 May to 2 June 17 BCE. Horace was asked to compose the festival hymn, the *Carmen Saeculare*, written in Sapphic stanzas and sung by a chorus of youths and maidens.

IV.7

Snows have fled away, now grass is returning to the
    fields and leaves to the trees;
earth goes through her changes, diminishing rivers
    flow within their banks.

One of the Graces with her twin sisters and the Nymphs dares
    lead the dance unclothed.
"Do not hope for what's immortal," the year warns, and the
    hour which plunders the day.

With the Zephyrs cold grows mild, summer tramples
    springtime, soon to die,
once productive autumn pours forth its fruits, and shortly
    lifeless winter is back.

Nonetheless swift moons repair their heavenly losses:
    we, when we go down
where devoted Aeneas, where rich Tullus and Ancus[1]
    are, we're shadows and dust.

Who knows if the gods above will add time tomorrow
    to the sum today?
All that you bestow upon your heart escapes the
    greedy hands of an heir.

When you at last have died and Minos[2] renders brilliant
    judgment on your life,

*Second Archilochian system*
    1. Tullus Hostilius and Ancus Marcius were two of the original seven kings of
Rome.
    2. A legendary king of Crete, Minos became one of three judges of the dead in
the Underworld.

no, Torquátus,[3] not birth, not eloquence, not your ✓
devotion will bring you back.

For from the darkness below Diana does not free the
chaste Hippólytus
nor is Theseus able to break through the bonds that
hold his Piríthoüs.[4]

3. Addressed in Horace's Epistle I.5 and perhaps the son of Lucius Manlius
Torquatus, consul in 65 BCE.
4. Hippolytus, son of Theseus, devoted to the chaste goddess Diana, died as a
result of rejecting the advances of his stepmother Phaedra. The Lapith Pirithous
(see also the end of Ode III.4) and his Athenian friend Theseus attempted to carry
off Persephone, queen of the Underworld, but ended chained to a rock. Hercules
freed Theseus, but neither Hercules nor Theseus could save Pirithous.

## IV.8

I'd happily present my friends libation
vessels, Censorínus,[1] and fine bronzes;
I'd give tripods, prizes of brave Greeks,
and you would not bear off the least of gifts,
if I of course were rich in works of art
which either Scopas or Parrhásius[2]
produced, the first with stone, the second skilled
with paint to represent a man or god.
But this is not my strength, nor does your fortune
nor your taste require such ornaments:
you take delight in poems; we can present
you poems and for my gift assign a price.
Not public records carved on marble slabs
through which the spirit and the life return
to worthy leaders after death, [not swift
defeats and threats of Hannibal thrown back,
not wicked Carthage all in flames][3] give praise
[of him who came back home when he had earned
a name[4] from his defeat of Africa]
more brightly than the Muse of Ennius.[5]
If writing does not tell of your fine deeds,
you'll not bear your reward. What would become
of Mars and Ilia's son, if envy's silence
stood against the worth of Romulus?
The merit, favor, and the tongues of mighty

*First Asclepiad system*

1. Gaius Marcius Censorinus, consul in 39 BCE or his son, who became consul in 8 BCE.

2. Scopas, a Parian sculptor and architect, active in the mid fourth century BCE, and Parrhasius, an Ephesian painter active in the second half of the fifth century BCE.

3. The bracketed passages are often considered to be later interpolations, which gloss the text. With two or six of the bracketed lines removed, the poem's structure accords with the rest of the odes, each of whose total lines are divisible by four—a feature of Horace's odes discovered by the nineteenth-century scholar Meineke.

4. Scipio Aemilianus Africanus (185/4–129 BCE) destroyed the city of Carthage in the Third Punic War in 146 BCE; Hannibal was defeated in the Second Punic War in 202 BCE by the first Scipio Africanus (236–183 BCE).

5. Ennius, regarded by the Romans as the father of Latin literature, celebrated the heroes of Roman history in his *Annales* and wrote an epitaph for the first Scipio Africanus.

bards snatched Aéacus[6] from Stygian streams
and set him in the Isles of the Blessed.
[The Muse forbids praiseworthy men to die.]
The Muse can offer heaven. Thus tenacious
Hercules is present at the longed-
for feasts of Jove, the Dioscúri,[7] shining
stars, snatch shattered ships from deepest seas,
and [with his temples bound with green vine-tendrils]
Liber[8] carries prayers to good result.

6. Father of Telamon and Peleus and grandfather of Ajax and Achilles, after death he became one of the three judges of the dead in the Underworld.
   7. The Dioscuri, Castor and Pollux, who were guardians of those at sea.
   8. Italian god of fertility, identified with Dionysus.

IV.9

Lest you perchance believe the words will die
which, I, born by the sounding Aúfidus,[1]
    give voice with artistry unknown till
        now, words mated to the lyre:

it is not so, if Lydian Homer holds
first place, that Pindar's Muse, the Cean bards,[2]
    Alcaéus with his threatening poems or
        grave Stesíchorus[3] lie hidden,

and time has not destroyed the playful verses
of Anácreon[4] and love still breathes
    and passion lives entrusted to the
        lyre of Aeólic Sappho.

Not only Sparta's Helen was enflamed
in wonder at a lover's coiffured locks,
    the gold flecked on his clothing, and his
        royal bearing and companions,

nor first did Teucer fire arrows with
his Cretan bow, not just once was
    Ílion beset, nor great Idómeneus
        alone or Sthénelus[5] fight

in battles that the Muses should extol
nor first did warlike Hector nor the fierce

---

*Alcaic stanza*

1. Aufidus River (the modern Ofanto) in Apulia empties into the Adriatic, not far from Horace's birthplace, Venusia (Venosa).

2. Simonides of Ceos, active in the later sixth and early fifth century BCE, and his nephew Bacchylides, active in the first half of the fifth century.

3. Greek lyric poet from Magna Graeca, active in the first half of the sixth century BCE.

4. Greek lyric poet from Teos on the west coast of Asia Minor, active in the later sixth and early fifth centuries BCE.

5. Teucer, half brother of Ajax, was the finest archer among the Greeks at Troy (see Ode I.7); Idomeneus and Sthenelus were other Greek heroes at Troy.

Deïphobus[6] sustain hard blows
    protecting their chaste wives and children.

There lived before King Agamemnon many
men of courage: but all unlamented and
    unknown are crushed in lasting
        darkness, for they lack a poet.

Not far from buried sloth is hidden prowess.
I through silence in my pages will
    not leave you unadorned nor will I
        let oblivion's dark malice

despoil with impunity your many
labors, Lóllius:[7] the spirit that
    is yours is prudent in affairs and
        upright in times fair and foul,

avenger of deceitful avarice
and shunning wealth that draws all to itself;
    a consul not of one year only
        but as often as a sound and steadfast

judge has preferred good to expedience,
it turns away with lofty countenance
    the bribes of guilty men and, victor,
        bears its arms through crowds opposing.

You will not rightly call a man of much
possessions blessed; more rightly he assumes
    the name of blessed, who can use wisely
        favors that the gods may offer

and can endure hard poverty and fears
a shameful act as worse than death, that man
    who for belovèd friends or country
        does not have a fear of dying.

6. Both Hector and Deiphobus were Trojan heroes.
7. Marcus Lollius, a wealthy partisan of Augustus, was consul in 21 BCE.

IV.10

O you still cruel and potent in the gifts of love,
when unforeseen your downy cheek confronts your pride
and hair which floats now on your shoulders will be shorn[1]
and your complexion finer now than reddest rose,

changed, Ligurínus,[2] will have turned to bristling beard,
"Alas," you'll cry, each time you see the other you
within the glass. "My heart today, why was it not
the same when young? Why will my cheeks not bloom once more?"

*Fifth Asclepiad system*
1. Boys wore their hair long but cut it on entering manhood.
2. See Ode IV.1.

IV.ii

I've an untouched jar of Alban wine[1] past
nine years old, I've in my garden, Phyllis,[2]
parsley to weave chaplets, I've abundant
    lushness of ivy,

with which, tying up your hair, you'll glow; the
house is bright with silver and the altar
bound with greenery craves sprinkling from a
    lamb placed in offering;

all the household servants hurry, here and
there girls mixed with boys keep rushing, flames
atremble agitate the sooty smoke in
    billowing eddies.

So that you may understand to what joys
you are summoned, you must mark the Ides,[3] the
day dividing April, the month sacred
    to sea-born Venus,

rightly mine to celebrate and near more
blessed than my own birthday, for from this
day my dear Maecénas counts the flowing
    years as they pass by.

Télephus,[4] whom you pursue, a lad not
of your class, a wealthy and a wanton
girl has overcome and holds him fast in
    fetters of pleasure.

Pháëthon, incinerated, frightens
greedy hopes and wingèd Pégasus weighed

---

*Sapphic stanza*
1. A fine but not a rare wine.
2. The name is suggestive of dark green leaves (Greek *phylla*).
3. April 13.
4. N-R in their commentary on Book III (238) comment that "the name Telephus
may have suggested 'shining far,'" from the Greek words *tēle* (far) and *phōs* (light).

down by earthborn Bellérophon provides a
    weighty example,[5]

that you always seek what's fitting and, by
judging it is wrong to hope beyond what
is allowed, avoid a match unequal. Come now,
    my last belovèd,

—for I'll not be smitten by another
woman after this—learn melodies from
me to render with your lovely voice—with
    song black cares lessen.

5. Both Phaethon, son of the sun god, whose fatal wish to drive the sun chariot
across the sky was fulfilled, and Bellerophon, who attempted to ride his winged
horse Pegasus up to Olympus but was thrown, illustrate the results of someone
overreaching himself.

IV.12

Now Spring's companions, breezes out of Thrace,
tempering the sea, press on the sails;
now meadows do not stiffen nor streams clamor,
    swelled with winter snows.

The swallow makes her nest, sad luckless bird
bemoaning Itys and a stain eternal
on the house of Cecrops, for she wickedly
    avenged crude lusts of kings.[1]

On tender grass the guardians of the fattened
sheep declare their songs to music of
the pipe and charm the god who loves the flock
    and black Arcadian hills.[2]

The weather's drawn our thirst, Vergílius.[3]
But if you long to drink wine pressed at Calës,[4]
follower of noble youths,[5] you'll earn
    it with a scented oil.

A little jar of oil will entice
a cask now in the warehouse of Sulpícius,[6]
generous to bestow new hopes and fine
    at cleansing bitter cares.

*Second Asclepiad system*

1. To avenge the adultery of her husband, King Tereus, Procne killed her son Itys
and served him to his father. On being pursued by Tereus, Procne was then turned
into a swallow or nightingale and Tereus, a hoopoe. Procne was the daughter of
Pandion, king of Athens, and thus the reference to Cecrops, founder of the Athe-
nian royal house.

2. Pan (= Roman god Faunus), the god of shepherds, was particularly wor-
shipped in rural, rugged Arcadia in the central Peloponnese.

3. It is a matter of dispute whether this Vergil is the famous poet or another,
unknown individual. By the time the poem was published, the poet Vergil was
dead, but the poem might have been written before his death.

4. A quality vintage.

5. Not being sure who this Vergilius is, it is not possible to determine his
patrons. If it is the poet Vergil, the reference would likely be to Augustus and Mae-
cenas, who were both younger men than he.

6. Probably a wine merchant.

But if you're anxious for these joys, come quickly
with your goods: I don't intend to steep
you in my cups without a fee, the way
    the well-stocked rich man does.

Put off delay and love of gain and mindful
of the funeral fires, while still you may,
mix with your plans a little folly: lack
    of sense is sweet at times.

IV.13

The gods have heard me, Lycë,[1] heard my prayers,
Lycë: you are getting old, but still
    you wish to play the belle and
        drink and frolic shamelessly

and tipsy rouse with quavering song the sluggish
Cupid: he keeps his vigil by the lovely
    cheeks of fresh young Chia,[2]
        skilled to play the cíthara.

For unobligingly he flies past dried-
up oaks and shrinks from you, for yellow teeth,
    and wrinkles and a snowy
        head of hair disfigure you.

No purple Coan silks[3] nor precious stones
restore to you the time which fleeting day
    has once enclosed and listed
        on the public calendar.

Where has attraction fled? Alas, where comely
movement, where fair hue? And what have you
    of her, the one, who radiated
        love and took my heart,

famed beauty, she of pleasing ways, my favorite
after Cínara?[4] Few years fate gave

*Third Asclepiad system*

   1. *Lyce* means "female wolf" in Greek, a pun on the Latin word for wolf (*lupa*),
which also is used for a prostitute (see also Ode III.10).
   2. "Chian Girl." Chios is a large island in the east Aegean off the coast of Asia
Minor and redolent of the voluptuousness of Ionia.
   3. Sheer silks from the island of Cos in the east Aegean were famed as a form of
provocative women's clothing.
   4. See Ode IV.1.

to Cínara, intending
　　to let Lycë long survive

to match the lifespan of an ancient crow,
that fiery youths might contemplate, not
　　without abundant laughter,
　　　　your bright torch collapsed to ash.

IV.14

Augustus, what attention by the Senate
or the Roman people, offering lofty
    titles listed in inscriptions
        or in annals, can forever

immortalize your merits, greatest ruler,
where the sun illuminates the settled
    shores? Lately the Vindélici,[1]
        who do not know our Roman

laws, learned what you can do in war. For with
your troops fierce Drusus, forcing heavy losses,
    overthrew the turbulent
        Genaúni and swift-moving Breuni[2]

and strongholds lodged atop the frightening Alps;
the elder of the two Nerónes[3] soon
    began stern battle and successfully
        repulsed the brutal Raetians;

O worthy to behold in martial combat
with what great destruction he assailed
    those hearts devoted to a death in
        freedom, almost like the South Wind

that stirs the untamed sea when the
Pleíadës part clouds, harassing tirelessly
    enemy formations, riding
        on his nickering horse through fires.

*Alcaic stanza*
1. The Vindelici were a Celtic and Illyrian people living in Raetia, which includes
the Tyrol and part of Bavaria and Switzerland.
2. Raetian peoples.
3. The Nerones were Nero Claudius Drusus and his older brother Tiberius Clau-
dius Nero (later the emperor Tiberius), the sons of Augustus's wife Livia by her first
husband, Tiberius Claudius Nero (see Ode IV.4).

For as the bull-like Aúfidus rolls headlong
flowing past Apúlian Daunus' kingdom,[4]
　　when it rages and contrives
　　　　appalling floods for planted farmland,

just so Tiberius destroyed the iron-
armored columns of the foe with huge
　　assault and, harvesting their ranks,
　　　　bestrew the ground, an unscathed victor,

when you provided troops, direction, and
divine support. For on the day that humbled
　　Alexandria had yielded
　　　　you her port and empty palace,[5]

now after fifteen years, again auspicious
Fortune's given you success in war
　　and granted longed for praise and glory
　　　　for performance of your orders.

The never quelled before Cantábrian,[6]
the Mede and Indian, the fleeing
　　Scythian[7] are awed by you, firm guard of
　　　　Italy and mistress Roma.

The Nile, which hides the sources of its waters,
and the Hister,[8] the swift-flowing Tigris,

---

　　4. The Aufidus (the modern Ofanto) was a river in Apulia emptying into the
Adriatic, not far from Horace's birthplace, Venusia (Venosa); river gods were often
represented in art as bulls. Daunus was a mythical king of Apulia.
　　5. Alexandria surrendered on 1 August 30 BCE.
　　6. A people in northwest Spain.
　　7. Like the Parthians, Scythian horsemen were wont to turn in retreat and fire
arrows at their pursuers.
　　8. Lower portion of the Danube.

and the monster-teeming Ocean,
   roaring at the far-off Britons,

the land of Gaul that finds no fear in death
and hard Iberia, all these obey
   you; the Sygámbri,[9] fond of slaughter,
      putting down their arms, pay homage.

9. Germanic tribe.

IV.15

When I had wished to speak of war and conquered
cities, Phoebus warned me with his lyre
    not to spread my meager sails
        upon the Tuscan sea. Caesar,

your era has returned rich crops to fields
and to our Jove restored the standards wrested
    from the Parthians' proud temples;[1]
        it has shut the gates of Janus

Quirínus,[2] now that wars are done; it's fastened
curbs to license overstepping ordered
    boundaries; it's removed wrongdoing
        and called back our ancient customs,

through which the name of Latium[3] and Italian
strength have grown, the fame and majesty
    of empire stretching from the rising
        sun up to its western dwelling.

While Caesar watches our affairs, no civic
rage or violence will banish peace,
    no anger forging swords and making
        enemies of wretched cities;

nor will those living by the mighty Danube
break the Julian decrees, nor
    the Getae,[4] nor the Chinese, nor the
        Scythians, nor faithless Persians;

*Alcaic stanza*
    1. These military standards were lost in the disastrous Parthian campaigns of
Crassus in 53 BCE and Antony in 36 BCE and were returned to Rome in 20 BCE
through a combination of intimidation and diplomacy.
    2. The closing of the gates of the temple of Janus Quirinus was symbolic that
Rome was at peace.
    3. The home territory of the Romans.
    4. Thracian tribe.

and we on days both sacred and profane,
amid the gifts of merry Bacchus, with
    our children and our wives, first having
        offered to the gods our prayers,

with Lydian pipes and song will celebrate,
the way our fathers have, our heroic
    leaders, Troy, Anchíses, and the
        progeny of nurturing Venus.[5]

5. Aeneas, son of Anchises by Venus, and his son Julus, ancestor of the Julian
line leading to Augustus.